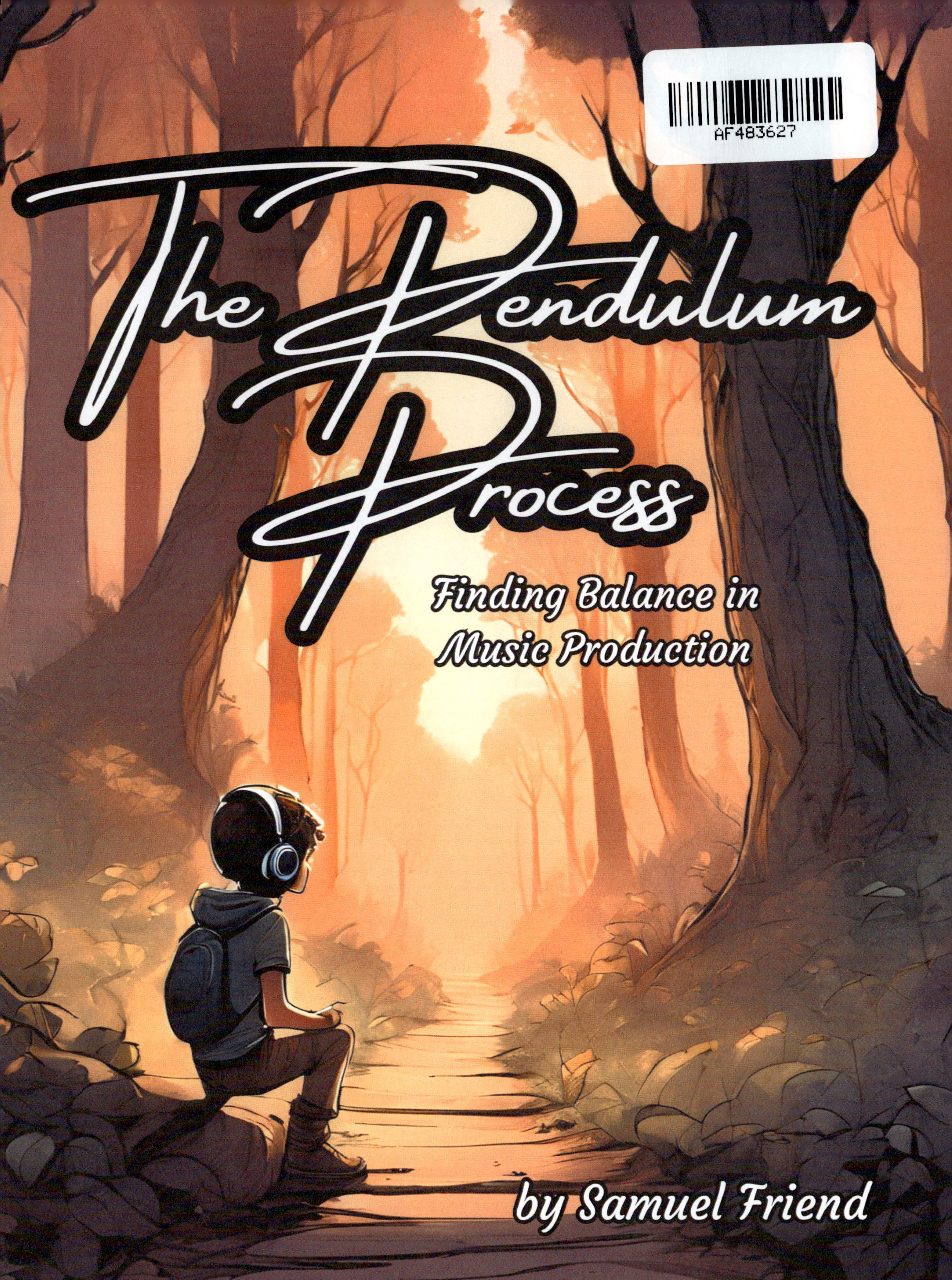
AF483627
The Pendulum Process
Finding Balance in Music Production
by Samuel Friend

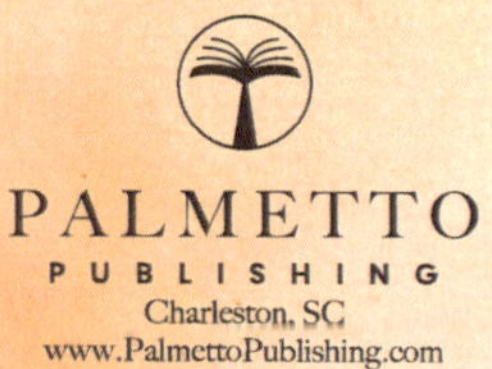

PALMETTO
PUBLISHING
Charleston, SC
www.PalmettoPublishing.com

Please note that much of this handbook is based on personal experience and anecdotal evidence. All concepts and analogies were created with the utmost honesty, and with the intent to inform and entertain the reader. None of the information in this handbook is intended to replace common sense, legal, medical or other professional advice. A reader is always encouraged to seek further information to gain a conclusive understanding of the subject matter. Any trademarks, service marks, product names, or named features are assumed to be the property of their respective owners, and are used only for reference. There is no implied endorsement if we use one of these terms.

Table of Contents

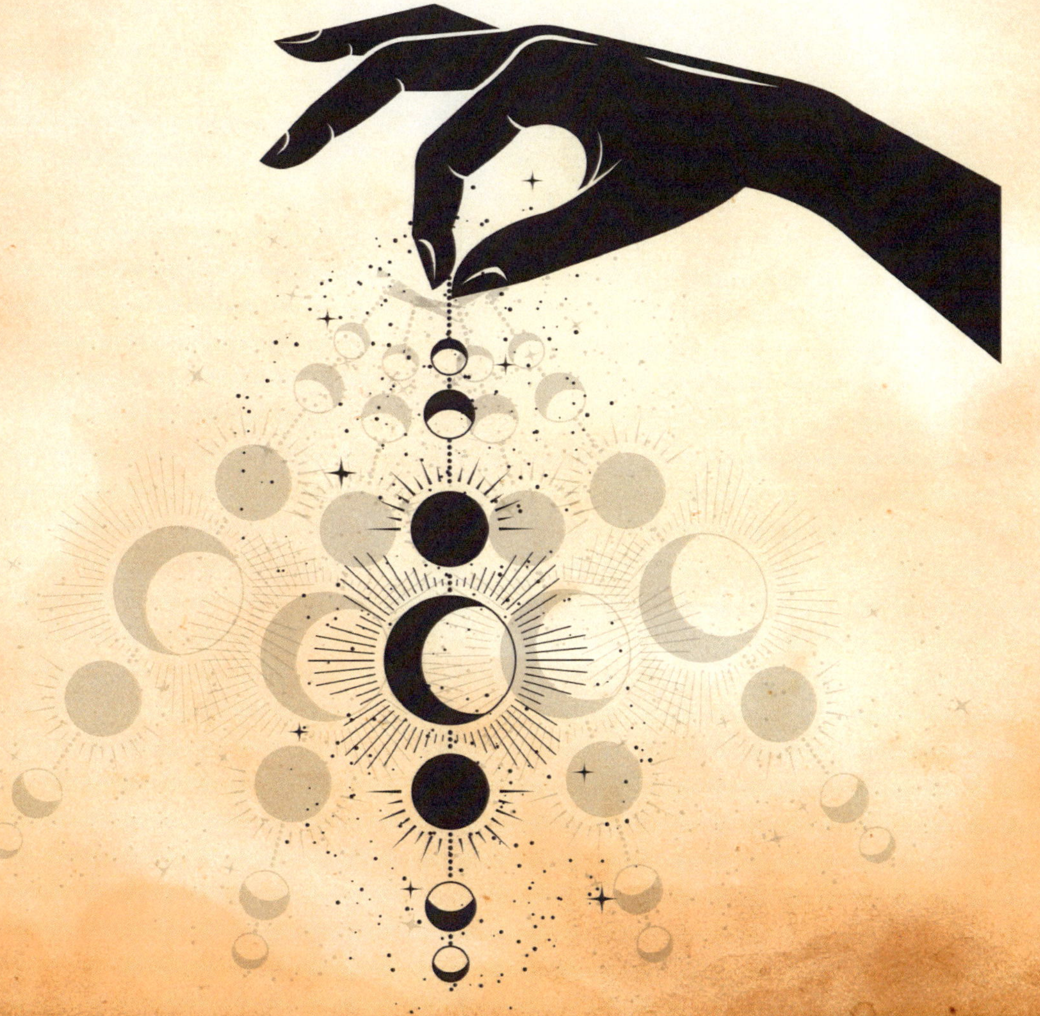

Welcome to
The Pendulum Process...

The Pendulum Process is the balancing act and intuitive force that allows a producer to make tasteful creative decisions. To make tasteful decisions, one must grasp the concepts of too much, not enough, and balance within a given context. The Pendulum Process enlightens the "myopic" or "short-sighted" producer. Remember, your goal as a producer is to preserve the "greatness" in great ideas.

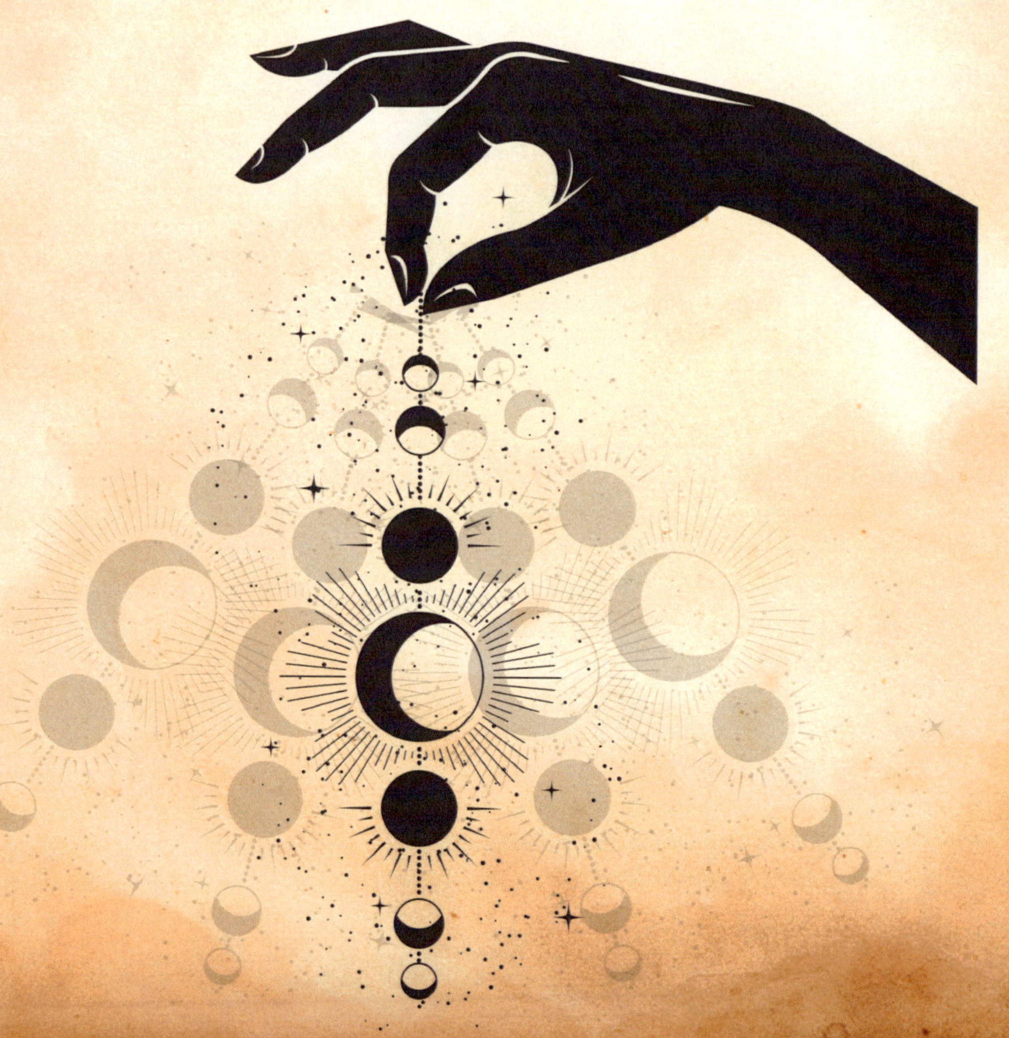

Learning the Map of Music Production

The method of learning Music Production is similar to navigating a theme park map. The more you explore the park, the better you'll be at creating the right experience. The sequence in which you explore is flexible, but ensure that you delve into and understand each area.

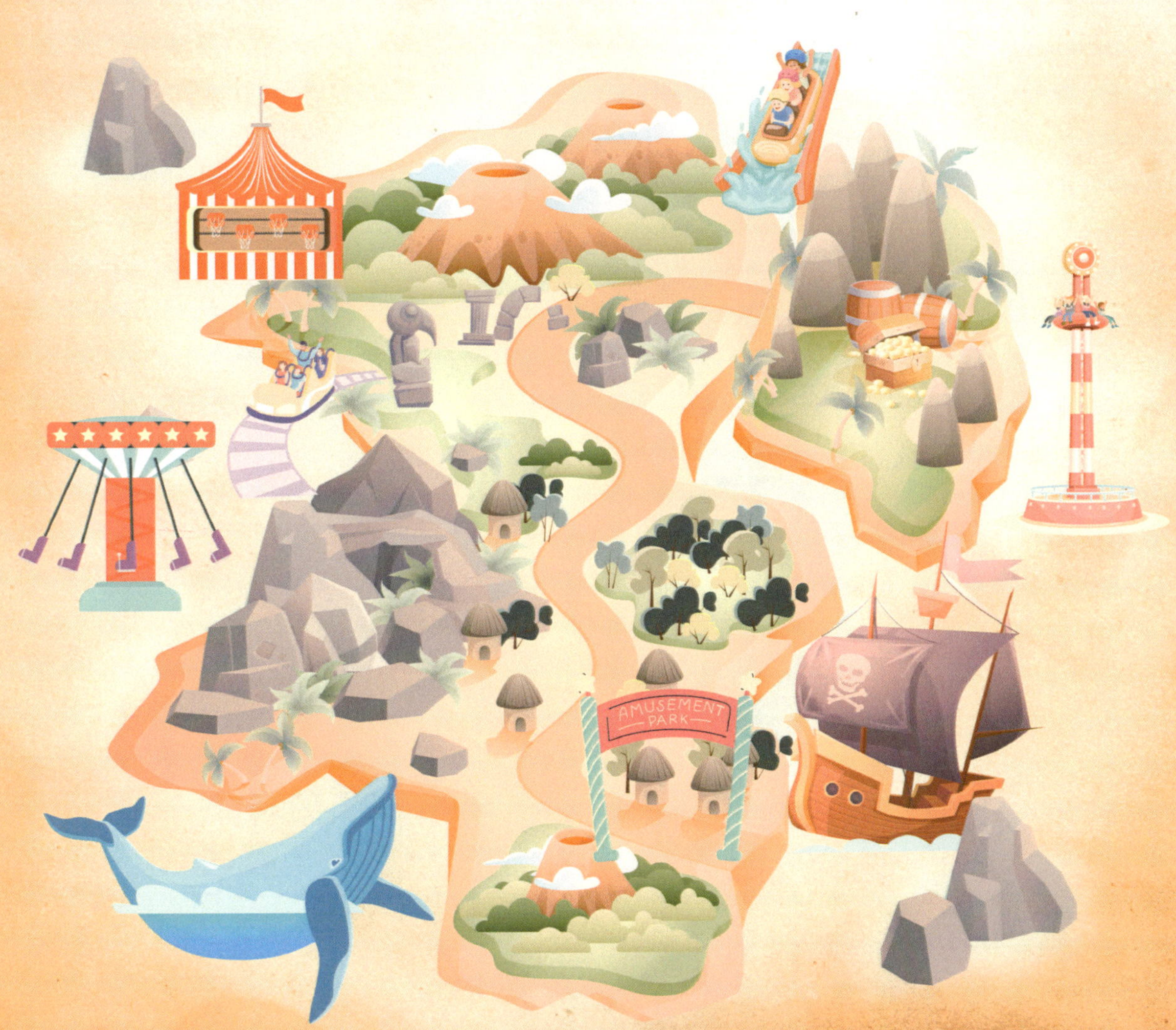

The "Big 4" Skillsets in the Pendulum Process

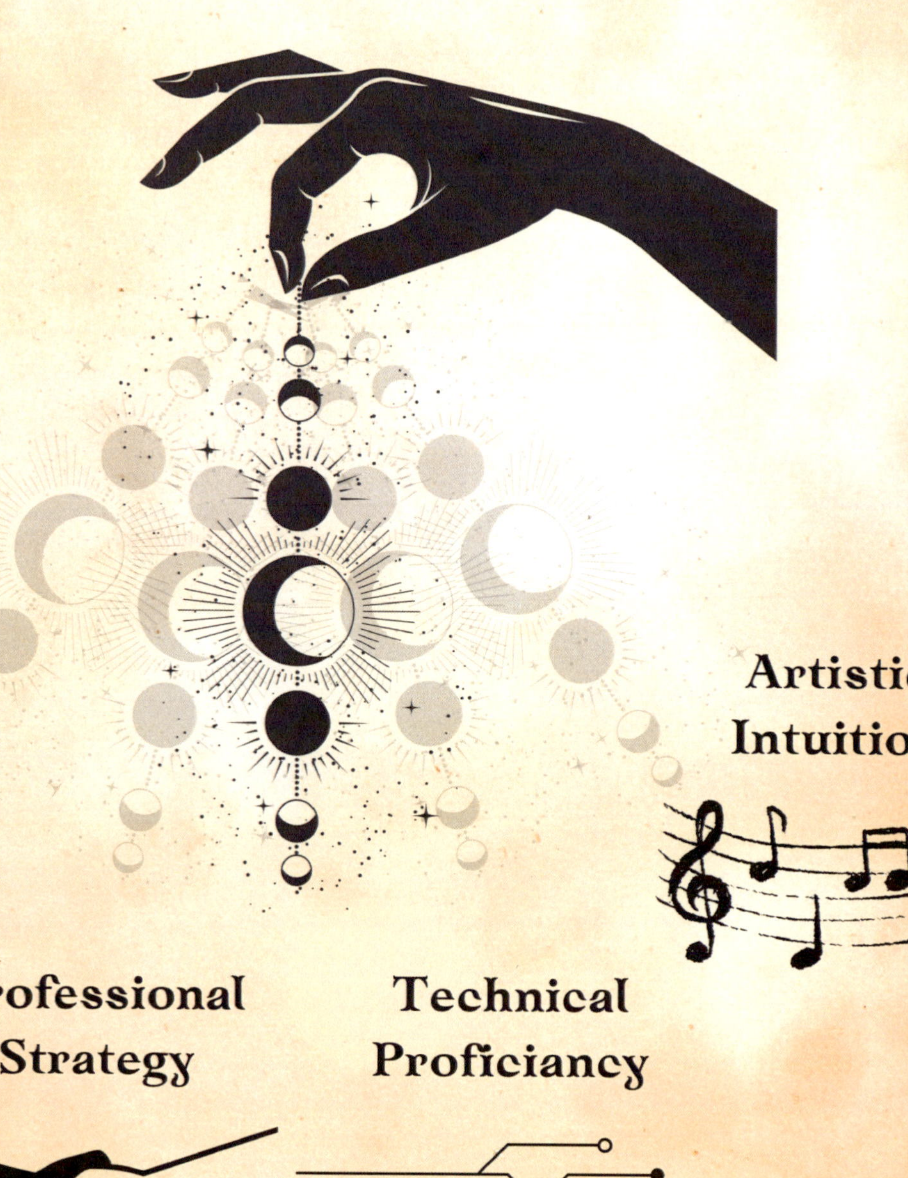

A balance of the "Big 4" will help a producer make tasteful decisions...

Feel the Pendulum Process

Ask yourself these 3 questions...

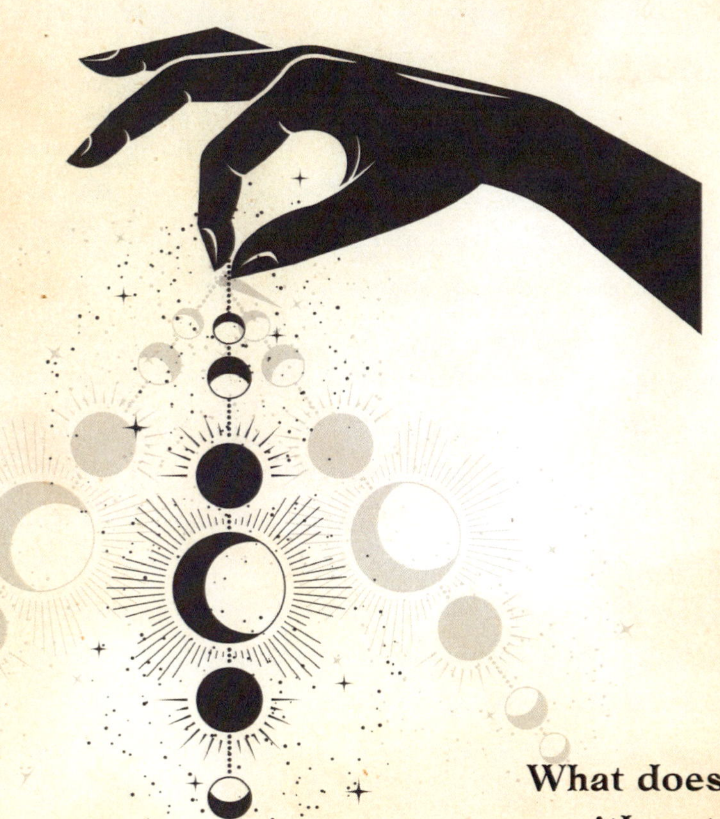

What does it feel
like with too much?

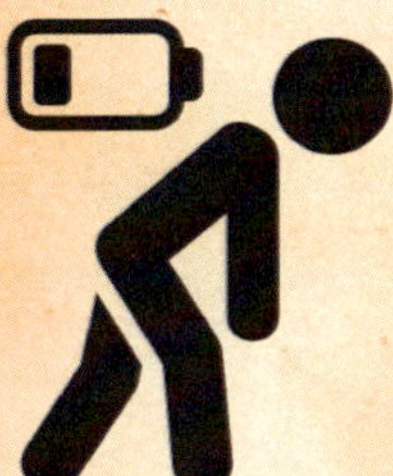

What does it feel like
with a balance?

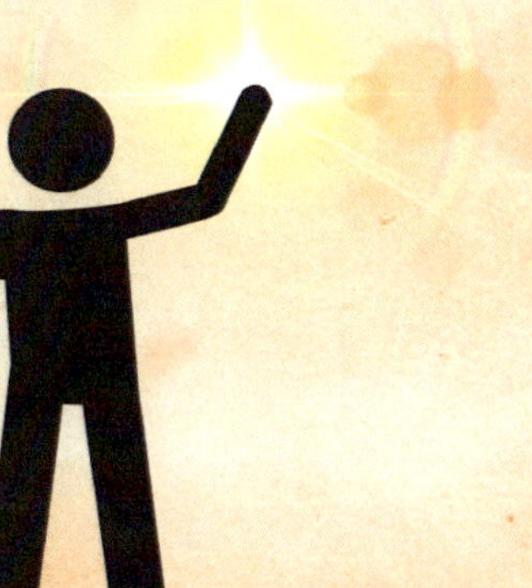

What does it feel like
with not enough?

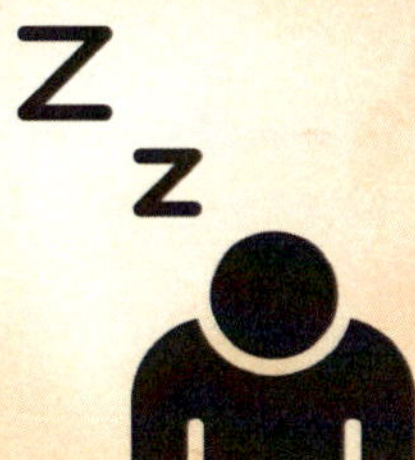

Too much of any 1 feeling can be boring or create tension...
Even a predictably balanced approach will become uninspiring...
A tasteful balance of all 3 will resolve this tension...

Concluding in the Pendulum Process

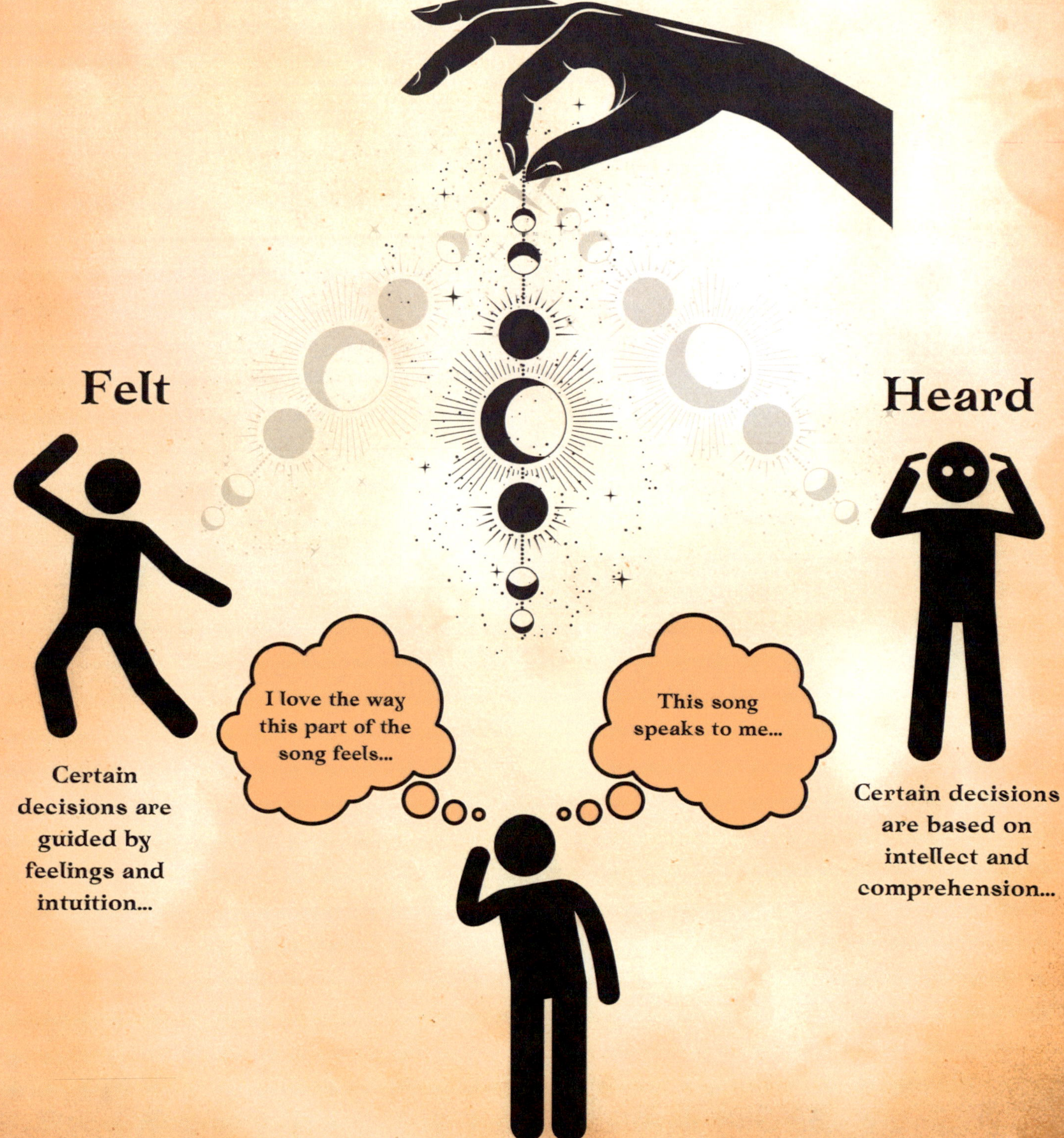

Awareness in the Pendulum Process

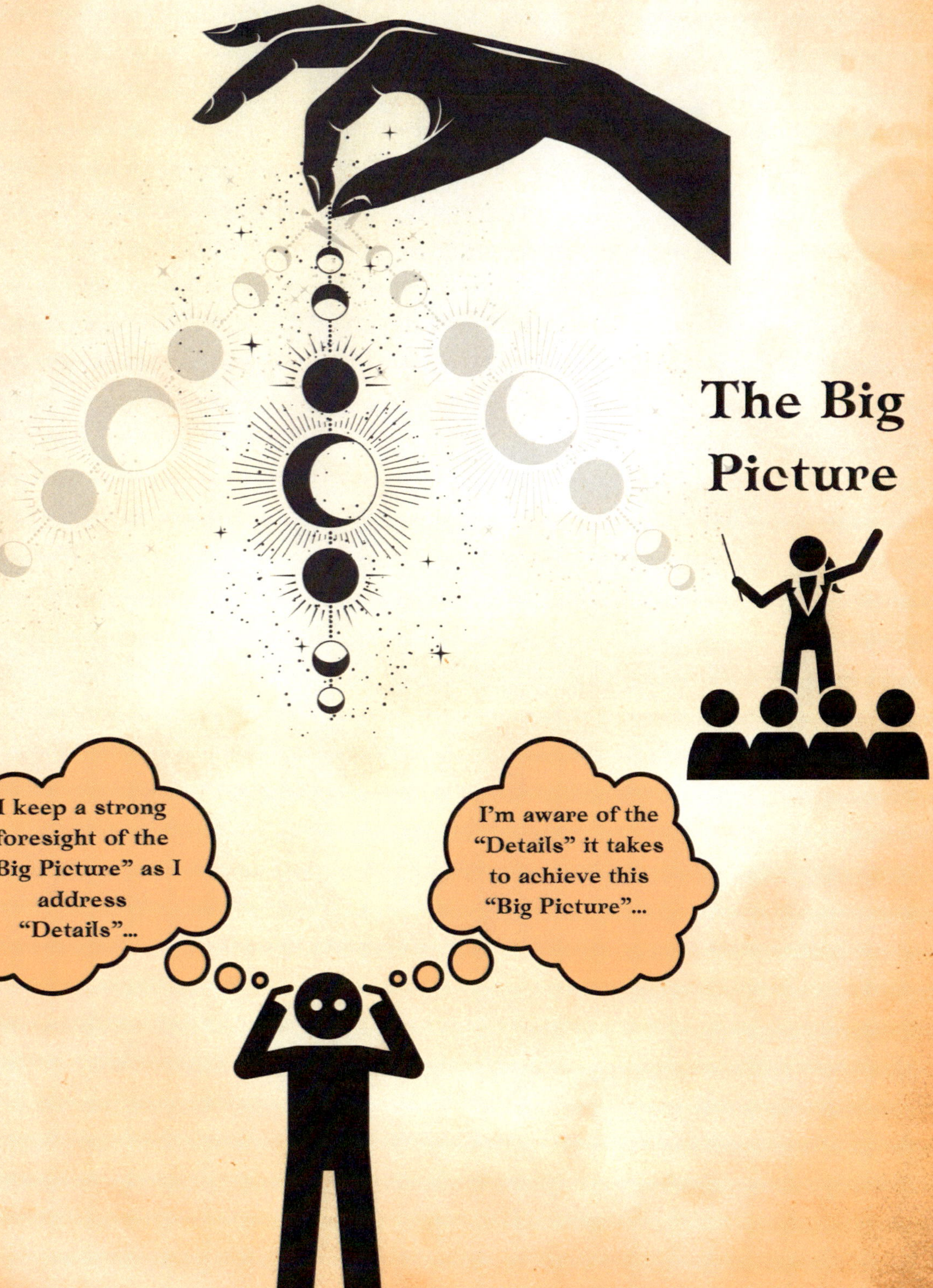

Producing in the Pendulum Process!

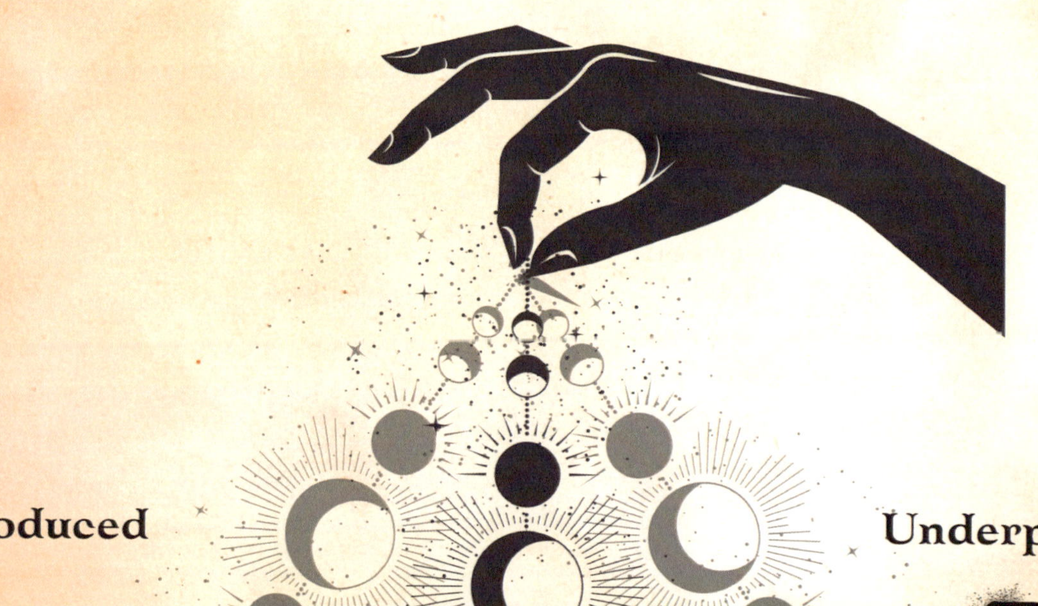

The fancy esthetic of a chandelier is similar to an "Overproduced" song. In this context, the aesthetic of the song becomes its central focus. While certain genres of music may require high amounts of production, if not tastefully managed, the result can feel lacking in humanity and authenticity.

Like a diamond in the rough, an underproduced song might initially seem to lack aesthetic appeal, yet with refinement, it can shine. If a song stays underproduced, it may hinder the overall impact of the song.

Creating in the Pendulum Process

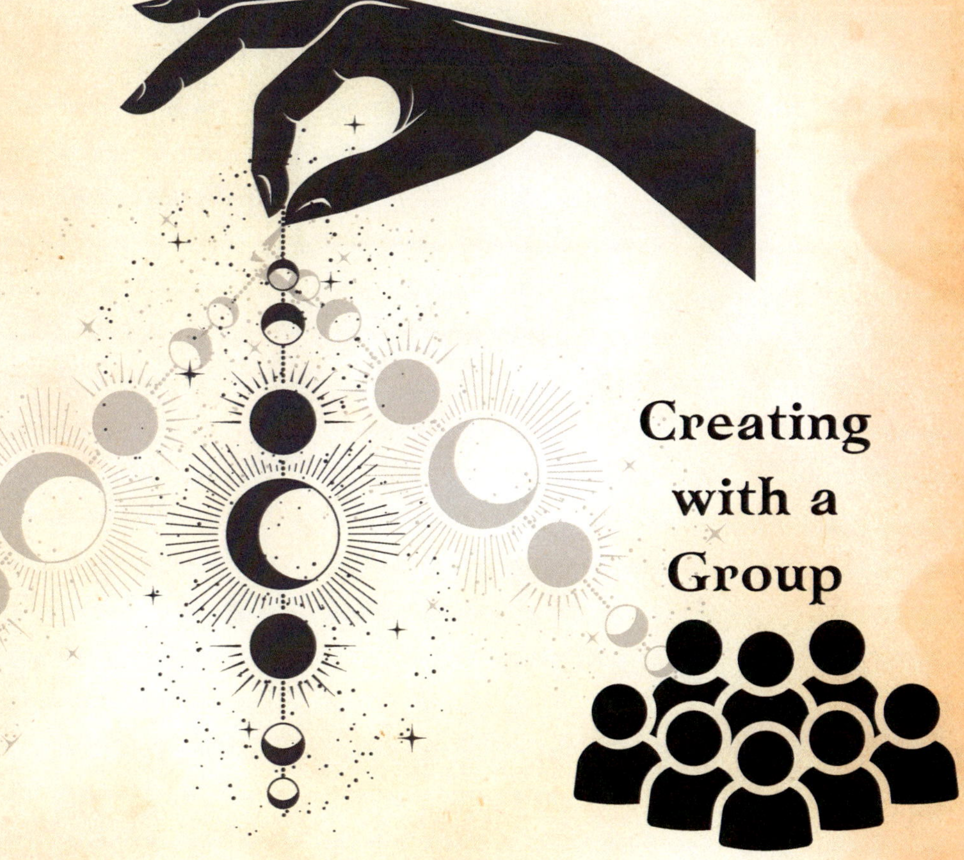

Creating Solo

When engaging in solo creation, individuals often adopt a more profound interpersonal approach towards the creative process. Songs tend to reflect deeper subject matter, and without the social pressure of a group, creatives tend to take more risks and show more vulnerability. This openness can lead to innovation, however the work load and pressure on a solo person comes with its obvious challenges.

Both individual and collaborative creation have their unique pros and cons. No matter which method you choose, a strong foundation of honesty and commitment is essential during your creative journey. By recognizing the natural tendencies of people, we can select the most effective environment for production.

Creating with a Group

You can also create through collaboration. Such productions typically reflect the consensus of the group, resulting in a collective sound that lends itself well in social situations. While this method helps distribute the workload and reduces individual pressure, it can also cause original ideas to become diluted amidst differing opinions and social pressures.

Committing in the Pendulum Process

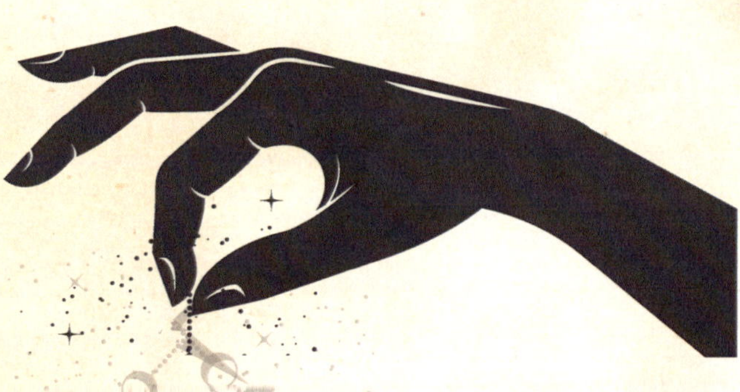

Commit to Yourself

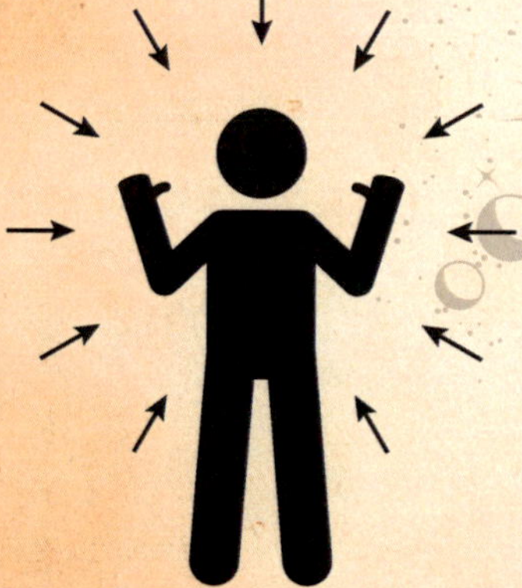

One of the most challenging tasks for an aspiring artist is to fully commit to one's authentic self. Self-expression can be a vulnerable endeavor, leading to an emotional rollercoaster. However, it's this leap of faith that is also one of the key factors in inspiring others.

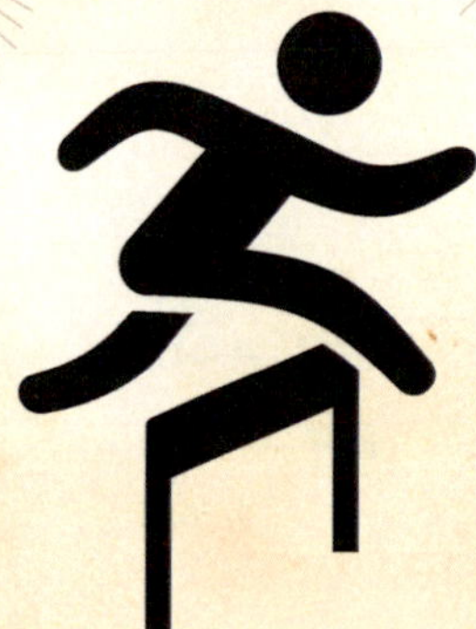

Regardless of style or genre, commitment to a performance is one of the only traits shared by all influential artists. However, several challenges can hinder an artist's commitment. These challenges may include inadequate preparation, feelings of insecurity, excessive self-analysis, or physical limitations. Therefore, focus on minimizing distractions and prioritize "commitment to a performance" over the pursuit of "perfection." Ironically, many of the imperfections will smoothen out naturally.

Commit to a Character

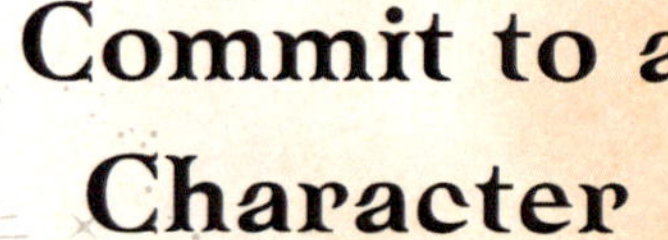

Often, an artist creates a persona or alter ego to help commit to a performance. This choice often serves as a protective barrier between the audience and the artist's authentic self. Many times, this character represents the artist's core values while keeping personal details largely undisclosed.

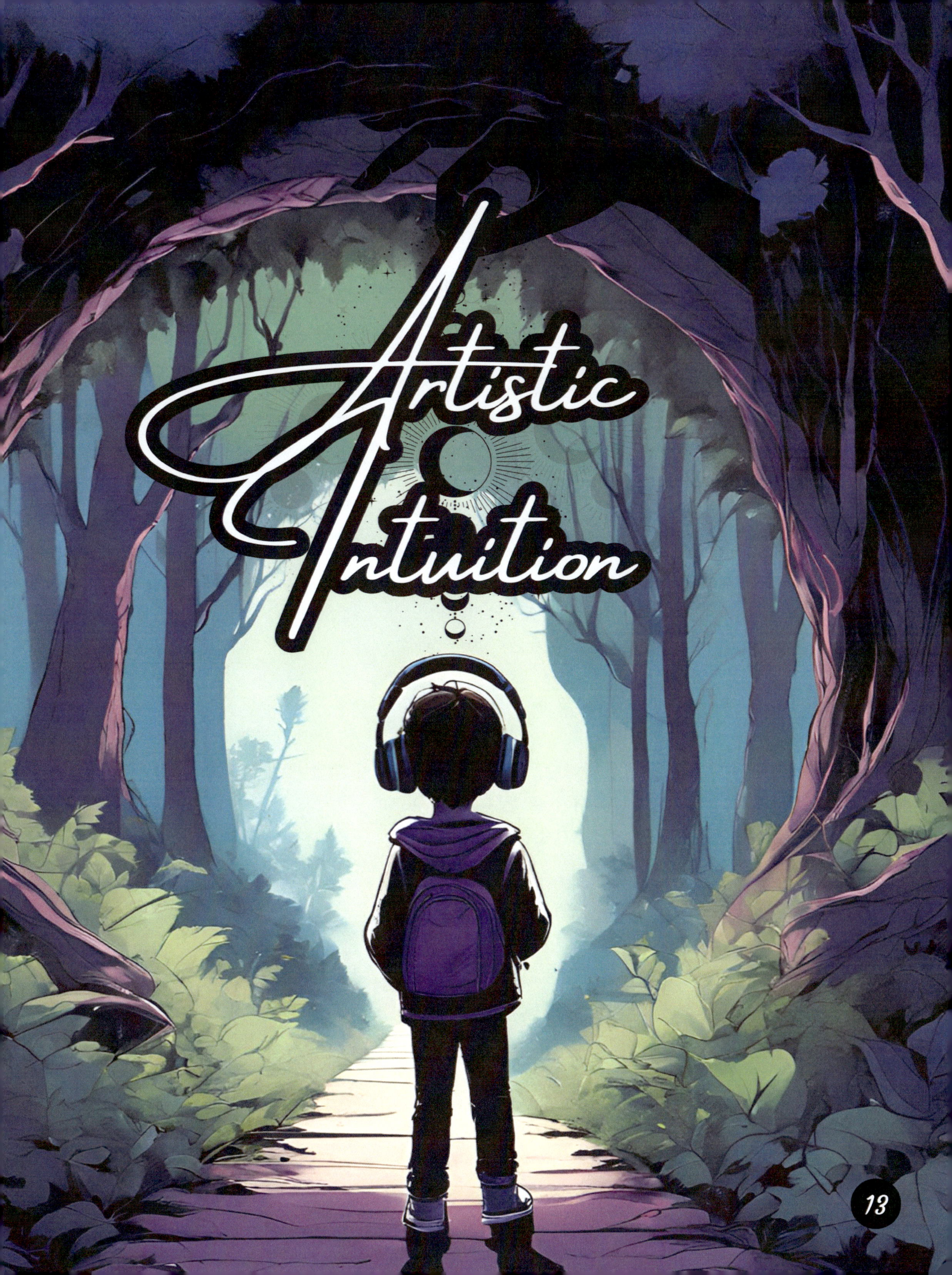

Artistic
Intuition

What are Your 3 Favorite Songs?

1. ______________________________

2. ______________________________

3. ______________________________

What is Your Favorite Moment of Each Song?

Song 1	Song 2	Song 3
Favorite Moment	Favorite Moment	Favorite Moment

What do your favorite moments have in common?

Explain what you have discovered...

"These moments are the foundation of your sonic thumbprint!"

Refer back to these moments for...

- ✓ Inspiration
- ✓ Creativity
- ✓ Self Discovery
- ✓ Burn Out Recovery
- ✓ Battling Uncertainty

By signing below, you are committing to staying connected to your musical inspiration. Amid distractions and challenges, it can be easy to forget what got you excited in the first place. This pledge ensures that your love for music remains at the core of your musical journey.

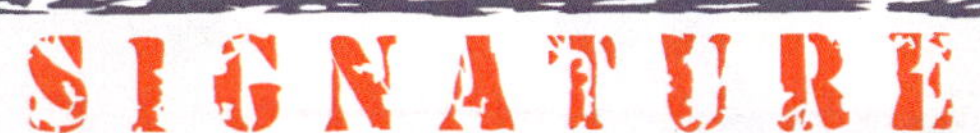

The 3 Phases of Production

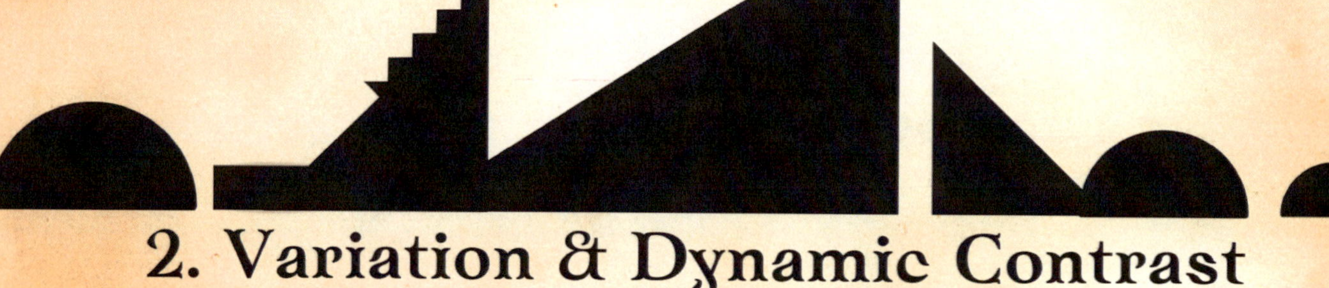

1. Emotional Road Map

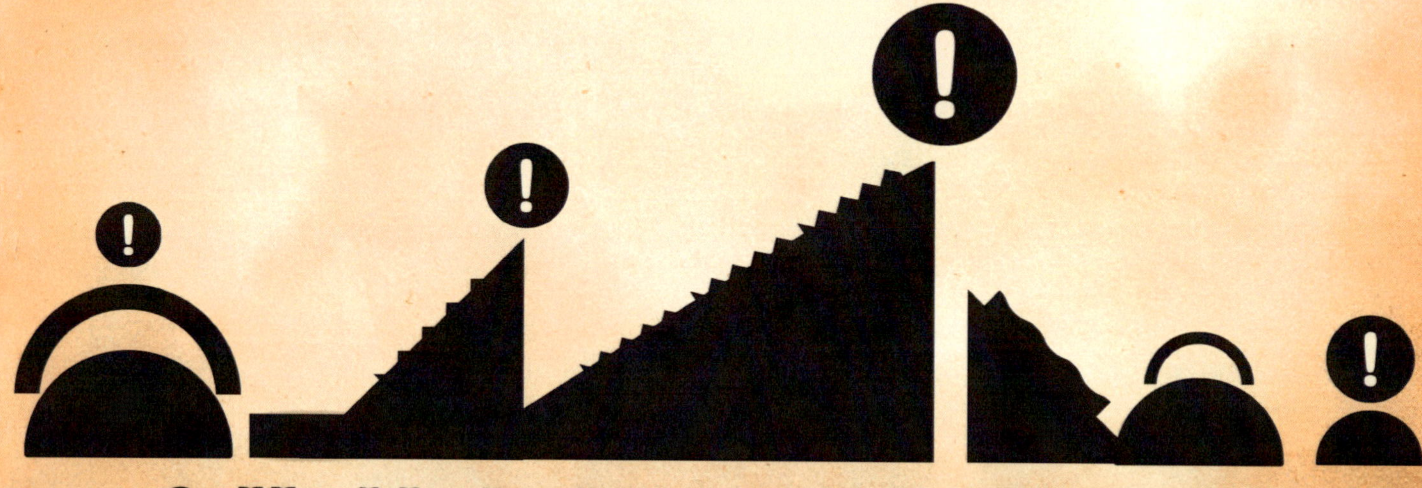

2. Variation & Dynamic Contrast

3. Highlight Memorable Moments

1. Emotional Road Map

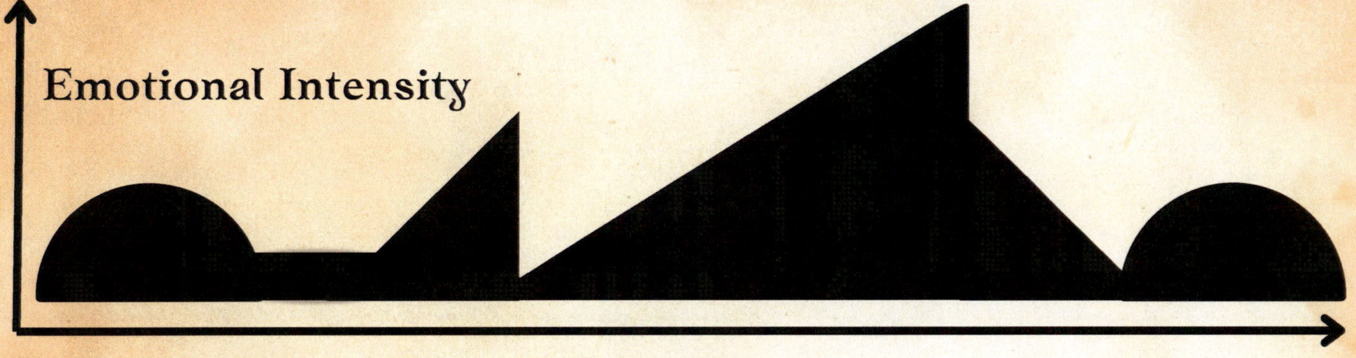

When you start to develop an idea, initiate the process by creating an "Emotional Road Map." Ask yourself, "What is the emotional journey of this song?" The abstract shapes illustrated above represent this concept. By gaining a clear understanding of the emotions that drive the song, you can make "tasteful" choices that align with that feeling. This approach prevents a superficial foundation and uncovers a narrative within your idea.

Additionally, it's crucial to establish a "big picture" perspective of your song as quickly and easily as possible. Each time you listen to your "unfinished" piece of music, you are essentially learning it "unfinished". This can increase the risk of writer's block, and complicate the completion of your project. The purpose of outlining a basic structure is not to confine your song, but allow yourself to hear your idea in a broader context. With this understanding, you'll have a clearer sense of what your music requires, and your initial ideas will remain at the focal point. Remember, this structure is merely a starting point, and you can adjust it as necessary.

Build a Hook
"Main Idea"

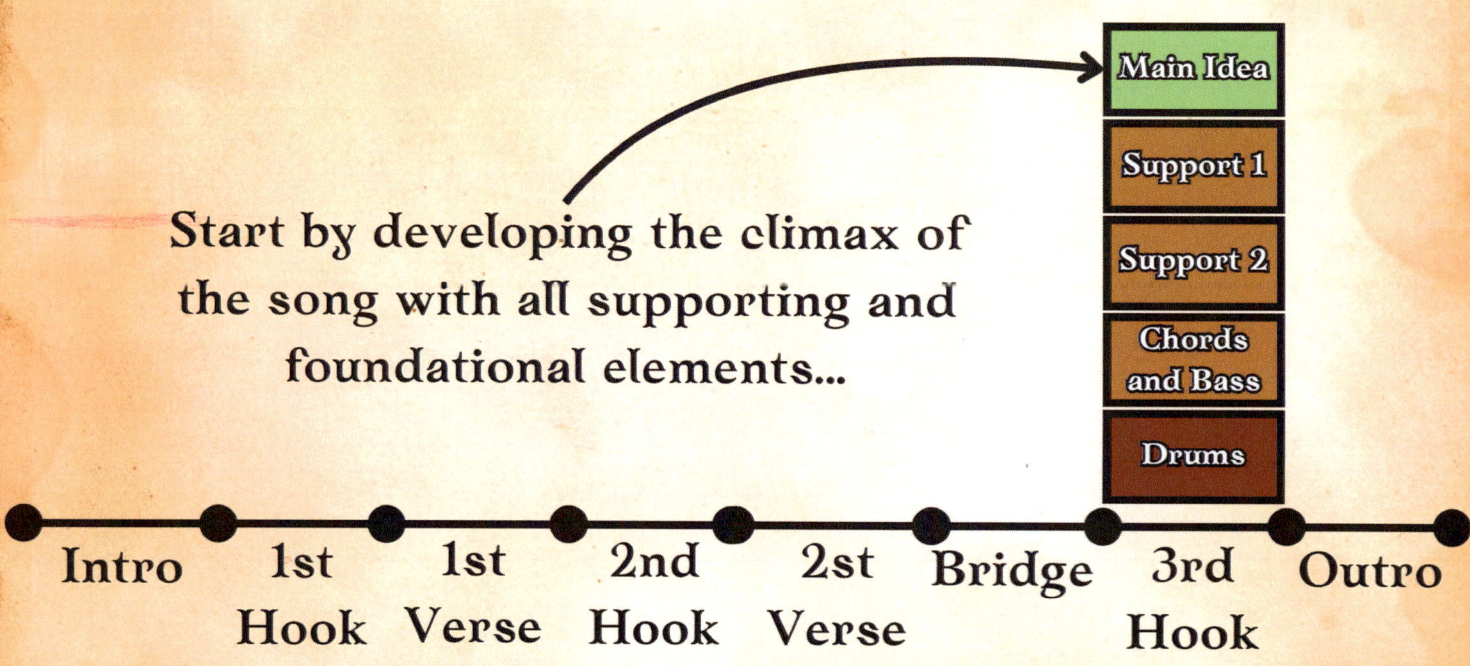

Begin your song by crafting a fully layered (orchestrated) "Main Idea" section that includes drums, bass, chordal instruments, lead instruments, and supporting textures. Consider this part of the song as the climax and position it as the 3rd Hook...

"Fly" the Hook

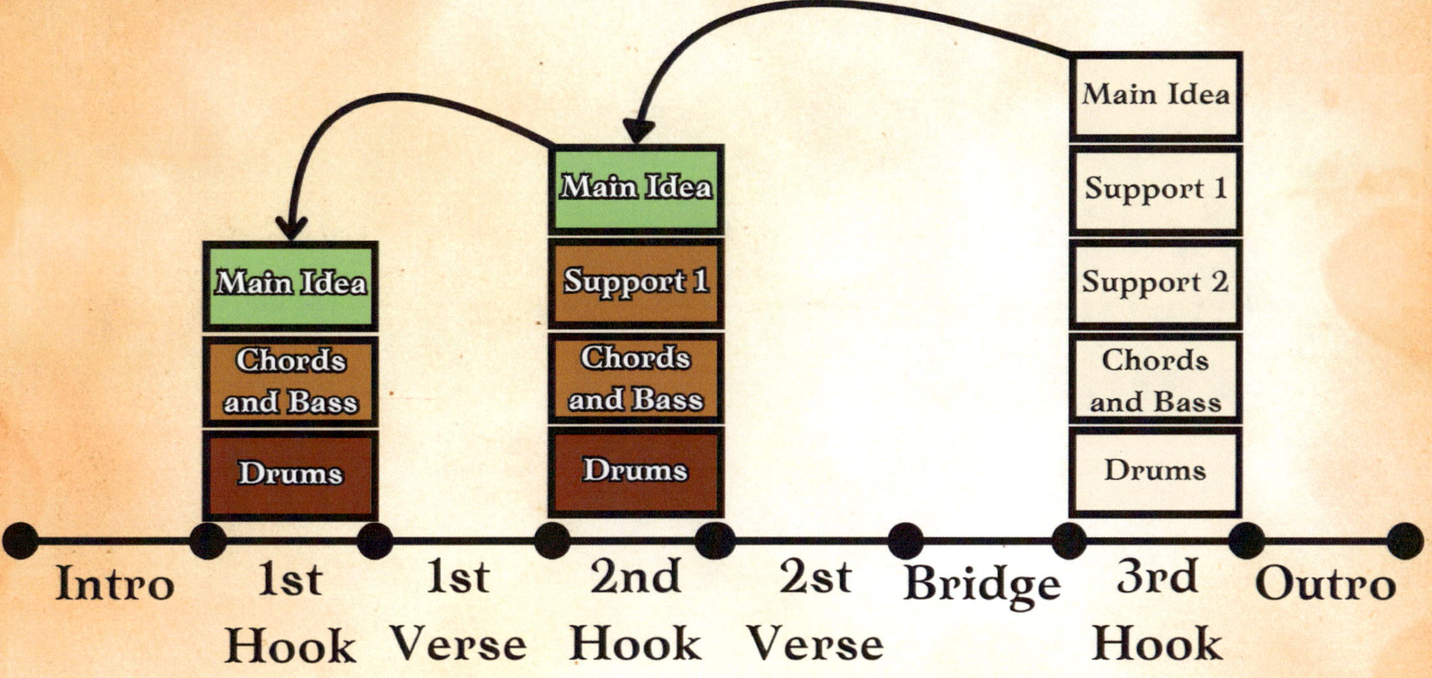

Copy (Fly) the 3rd Hook to the 2nd and 1st Hook spots. For the 1st Hook, remove all supporting elements, keeping only the core elements of your initial idea...

Finally, strike a balance between the 1st and 3rd Hooks to generate a feeling of progression and crescendo leading to the climax of the song...

Building your Verses

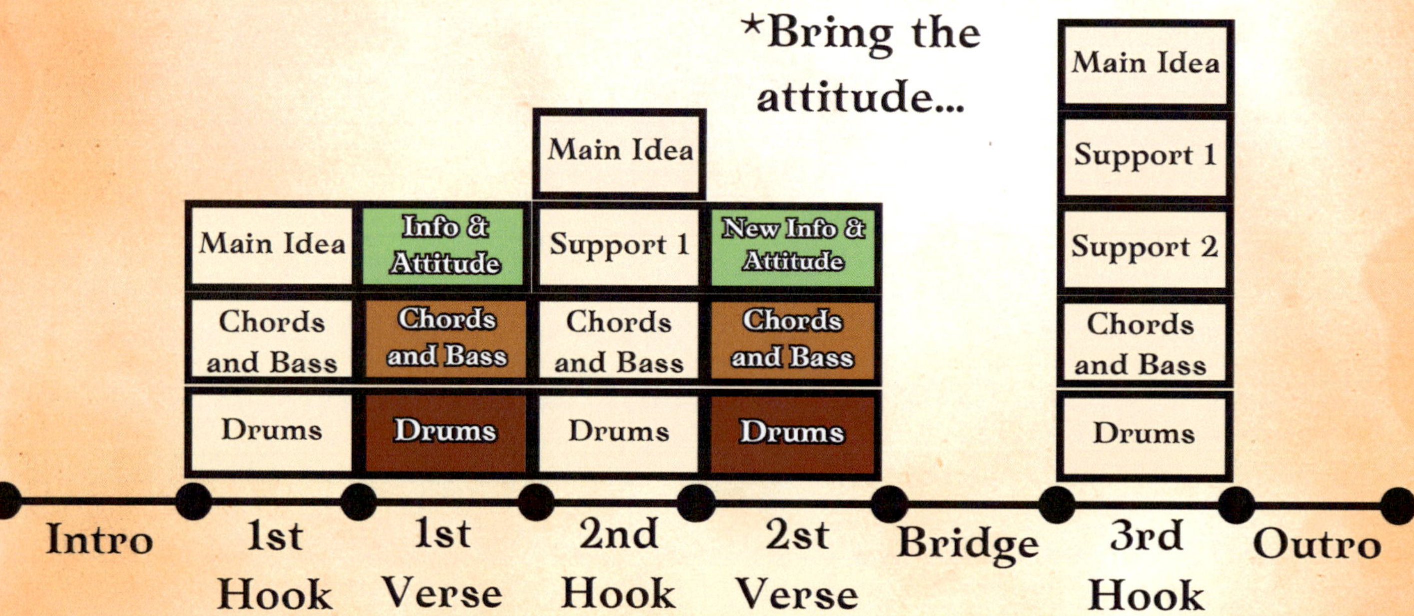

Copy the drums, bass, and chordal components from the hook into the verses. Limit the use of melody to redirect the song's emphasis towards the lyrical content. For a more pronounced musical contrast, consider adding entirely new elements like chords, rhythms, or textures, but keep them simpler than the hook. Lastly, use the verse to inform the listener, and determine the song's attitude.

Add an Intro & Outro

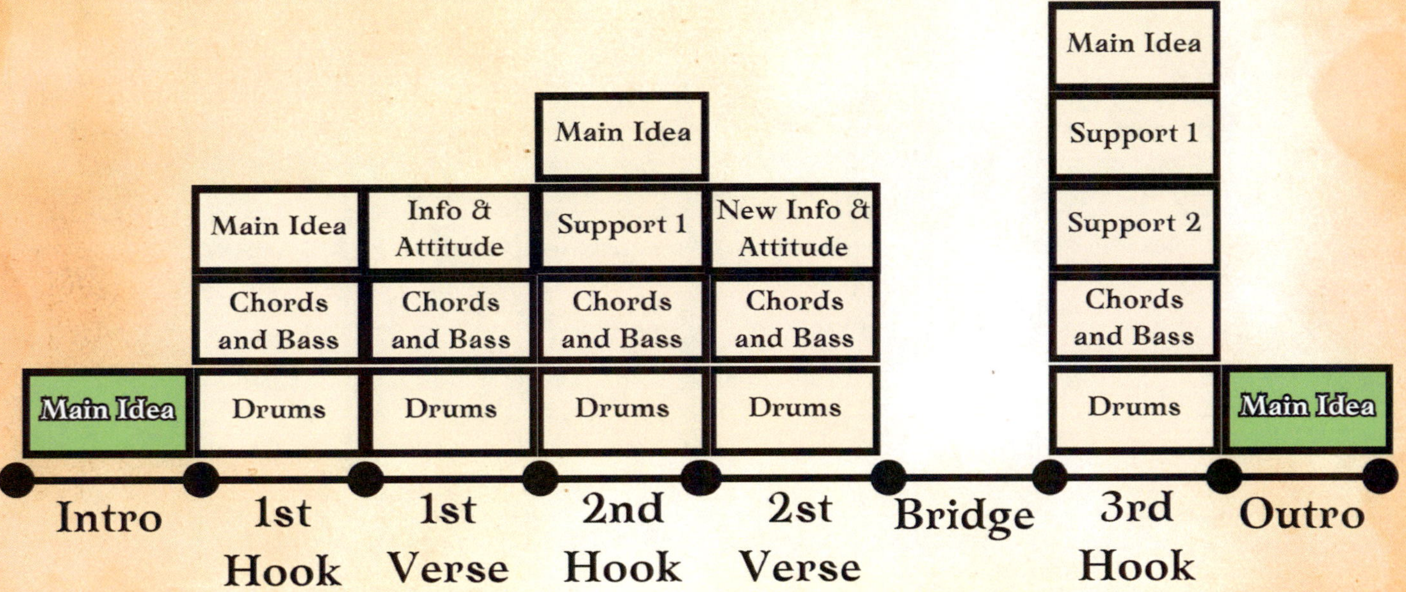

Incorporate a simplified version of your main theme into both the introduction and conclusion of the song. Additionally, consider using supportive textures to enhance the overall sound.

Add a Bridge

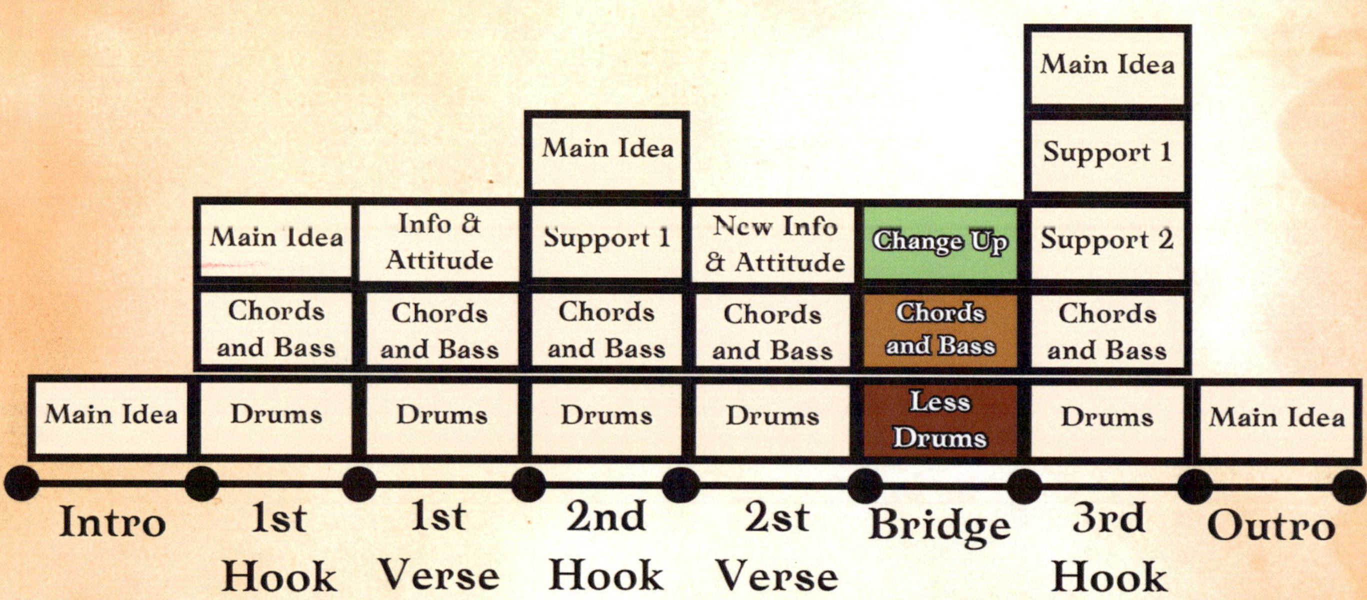

When crafting the bridge, it's essential to introduce a contrasting concept from your main idea. This segment within a song serves to add variety and break up any repetition in the music. If the song contains consistent rhythm and drums, consider changing the rhythmic feel or eliminate the drums all together.

Basic Song Structure!

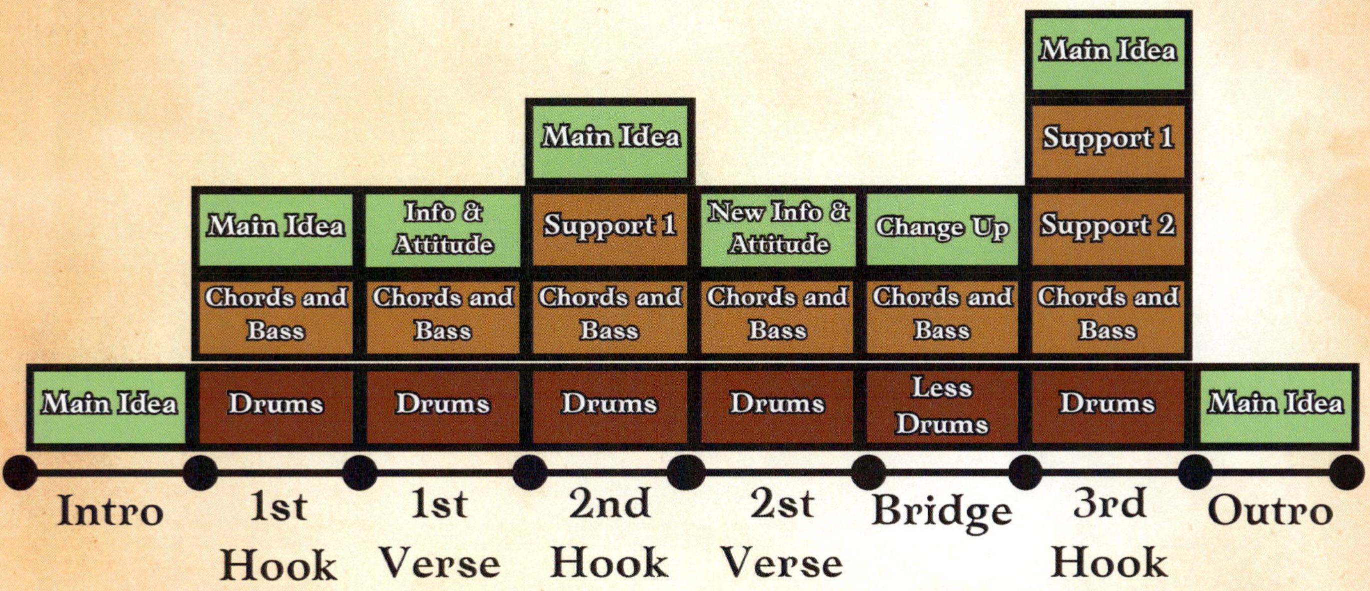

Remember, this song structure is intentionally simple, predictable, and marks the initial stage of your production. By quickly transforming your main idea into a basic song, you allow yourself to gain a "big picture" perspective of your main idea. This gives you clearer judgment on a plan of action and helps avoid writer's block...

*In many ways, song structure reflects patterns in behavior and the human condition...

How many reflections can you discover?

2. Variation & Dynamic Contrast

After setting up a foundation, the next step is to introduce diversity and dynamic contrast to your music. This is where you can incorporate intriguing modifications and variations to your concepts. While there are no strict rules or boundaries, it's essential to explore the balance between tension and resolution. Remember, even the best idea can become stale if used excessively, so don't hesitate to experiment and introduce variety. For ideas, refer to the "Musical Tug of War".

Musical Tug of War

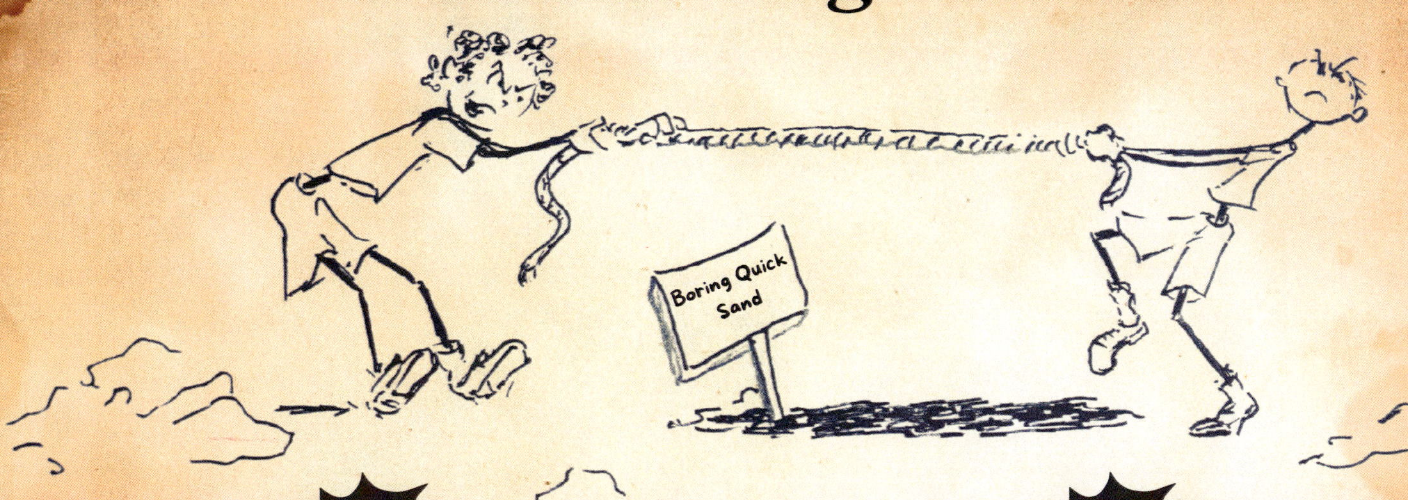

Long Note	Short Note	Straight Time	Odd Time
Chords with Tension	Chords with Resolution	Fast Rhythm	Slow Rhythm
Lo-Fi	Hi-Fi	Bright Mix	Dark Mix
Narrow Sound	Wide Sound	Hi Hat Groove	Ride Groove
Direct Sound	Ambient Sound	Cut Time	Half Time
Up Beats	Down Beats	"Mid Rangy" Sound'	Scooped Mid Range
Heavy Sound	Soft Sound	Improvised	Rehearsed
Male Voice	Female Voice	Organic Sound	Synthesized Sound
Melodic	Textural	Close Sound	Far Sound
Felt	Heard	Simple Sound	Complex Sound
Risky Lyrics	Safe Lyrics	Sub Frequencies	Air Frequencies
Tiplet Feel	Duplet Feel	High Energy	Low Energy
High Note	Low Note	Harsh Sound	Muddy Sound
Original Composition	Remixed Composition	Instrumental	Acapella
Rising Melodic Line	Falling Melodic Line	Predictable	Un-Predictable
Sound	Silence	Repetative	Through Composed

Music in the Pendulum Process!

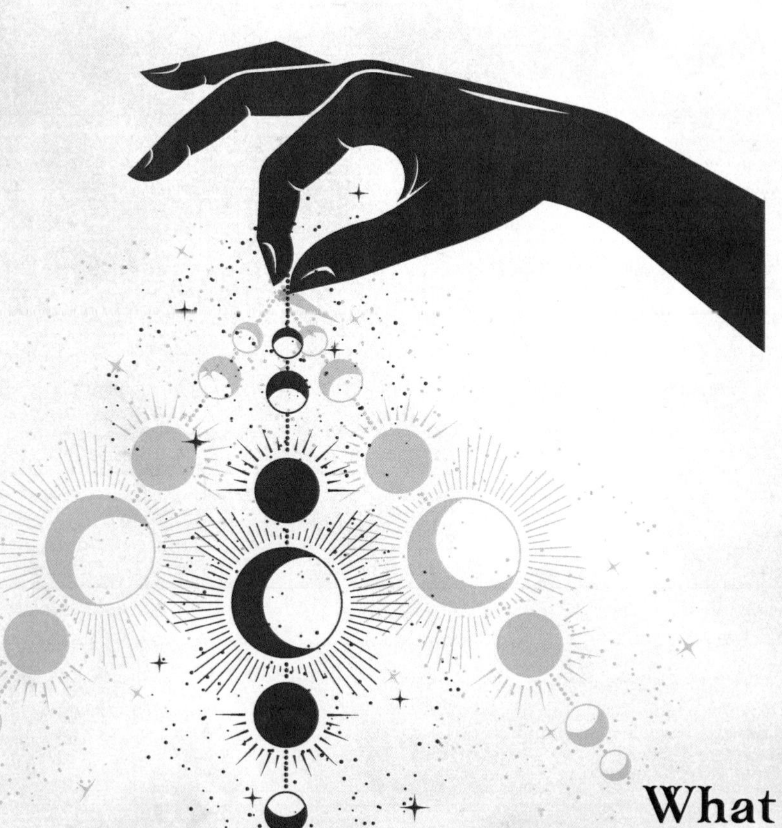

What does it sound like with too much tension?

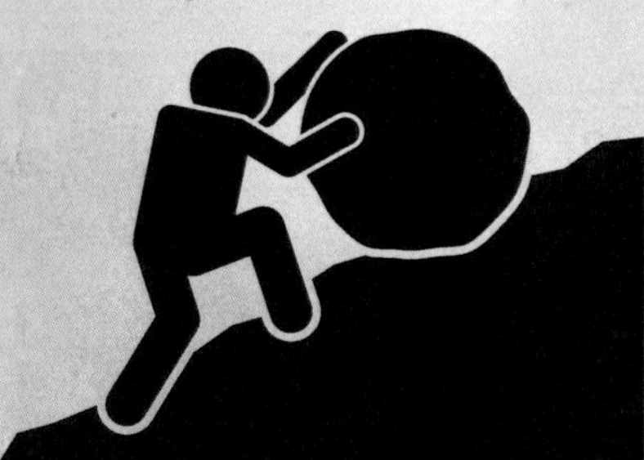

What does it sound like with a balance of tension and resolution?

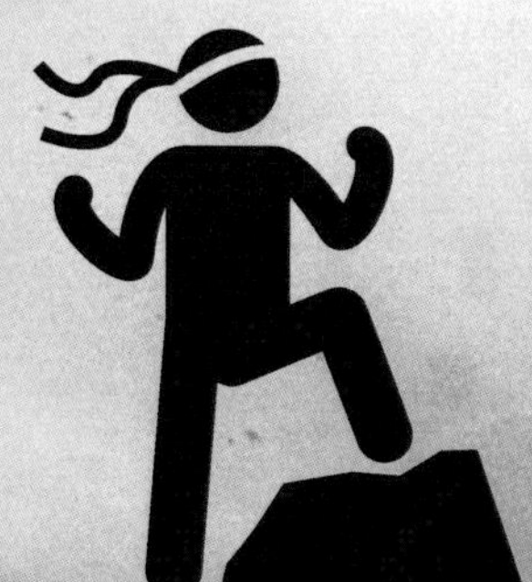

What does it sound like with too much resolusion?

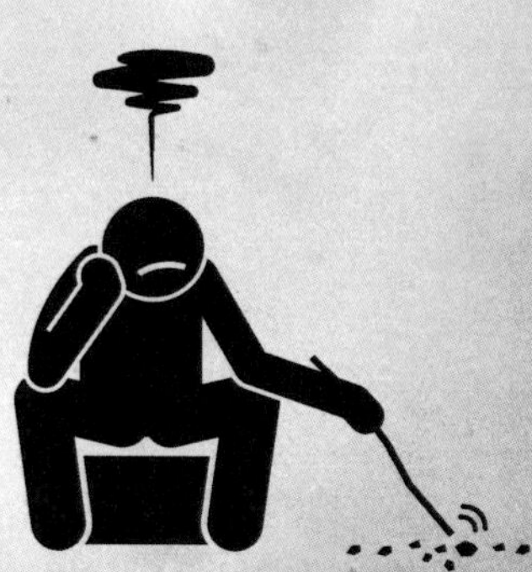

3. Highlight Memorable Moments

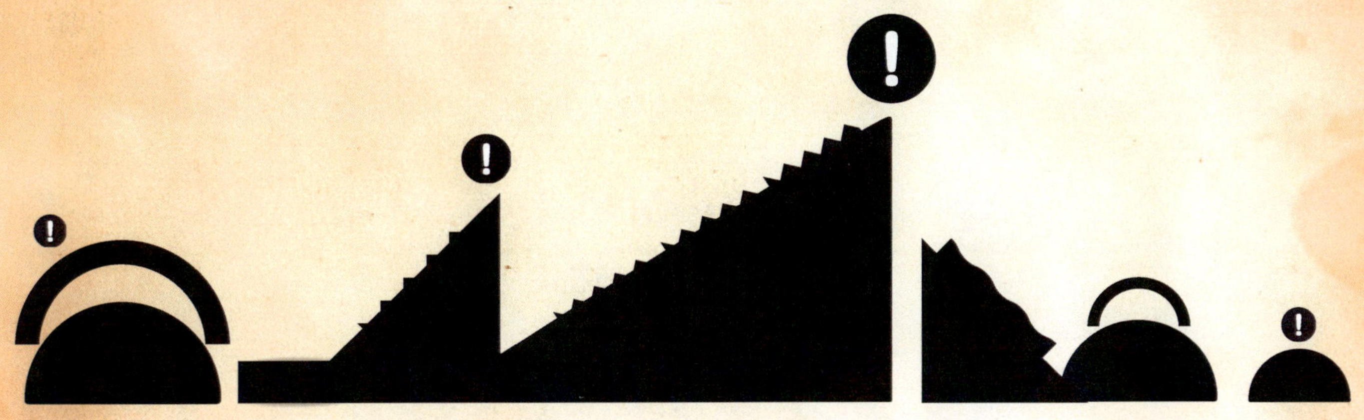

At the third and final stage of production, the focus shifts towards highlighting "moments". Once you have developed variations and dynamic contrasts, it becomes crucial to revisit the core idea of your music and enhance the memorable segments you want the audience to remember. Stay bold and ensure the main idea of your song remains crystal clear.

Classic Tricks to Highlight Moments!

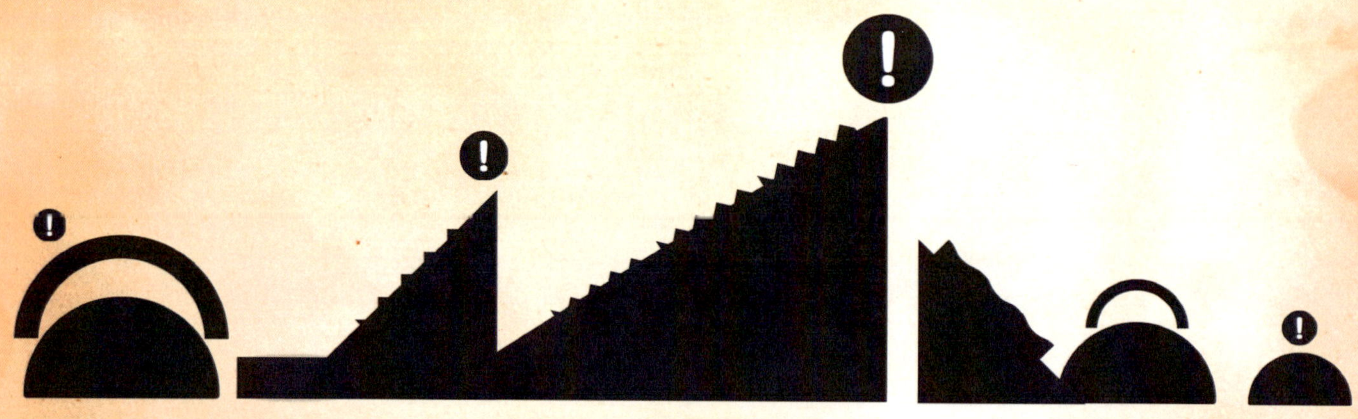

1. Double check there are no sonic elements in the sound foreshadowing the "Moment"...
2. Focus on what happens before the "Moment"...
3. Use special textures to add sonic interest...
   Ex: Drop Outs, Reverses, Filtered Sounds, Re-Mix FX, Delay Throws, Reverb Blasts, etc...
4. Focus on what happens after the "Moment"...
5. Tastefully reprise but don't overuse "Moments"...
6. GO BOLD!!

The Classic Filter Trick!

An easy way to create a quick moment is to alter a clip of audio using an AudioSuite plugin... This is the type of processing that will "bake" the effect into the clip...

1 Select the desired clip...

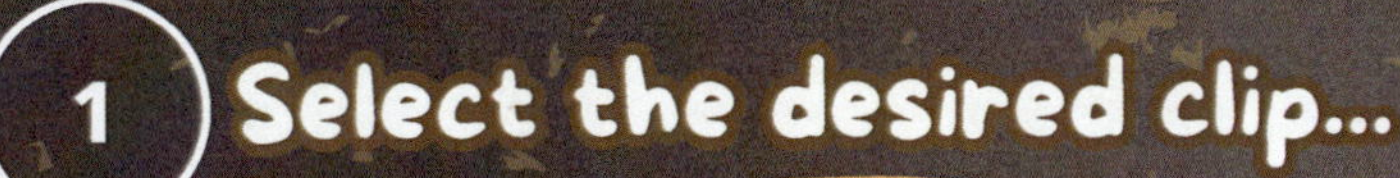

2 Choose the desired AudioSuite plugin...

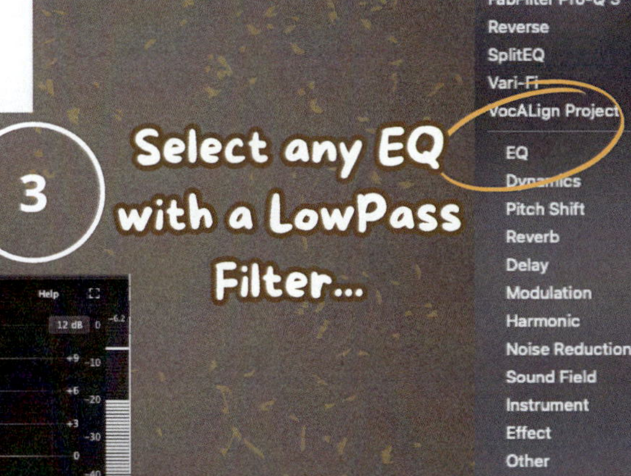

3 Select any EQ with a LowPass Filter...

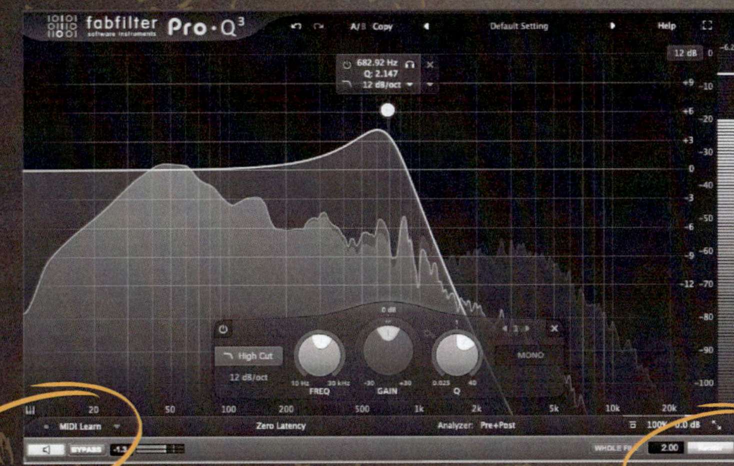

4 Select the speaker icon on the bottom left corner to audition the effect...

5 Once you are happy with the sound, click "Render" on the bottom right corner, and the effect will "bake" into the audio clip...

The Classic Reverse Reverb Trick!

1 Select a clip...

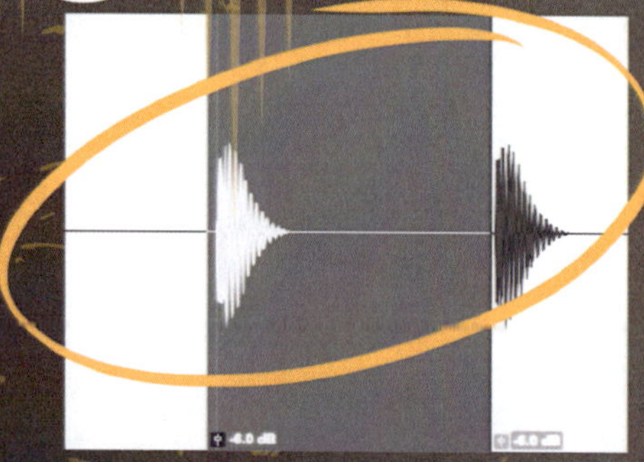

2 Choose a Reverb AudioSuite and render the clip...

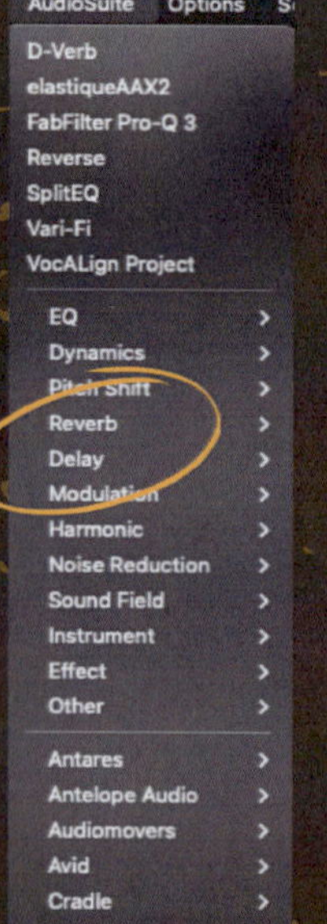

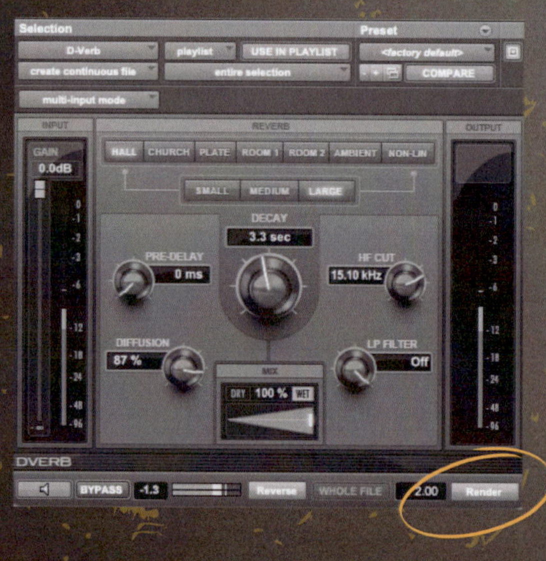

3 Select the rendered "Reverb" sound...

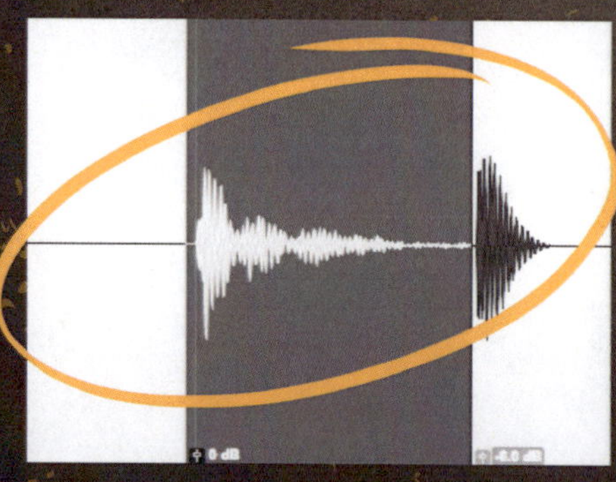

4 Choose the Reverse AudioSuite and render the clip...

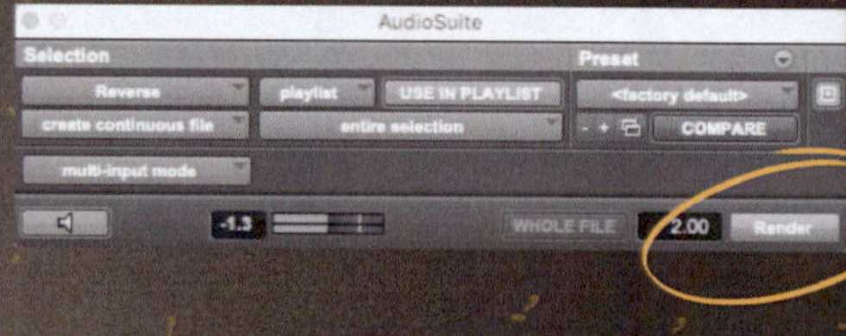

5 Refine the reverse clip timing...

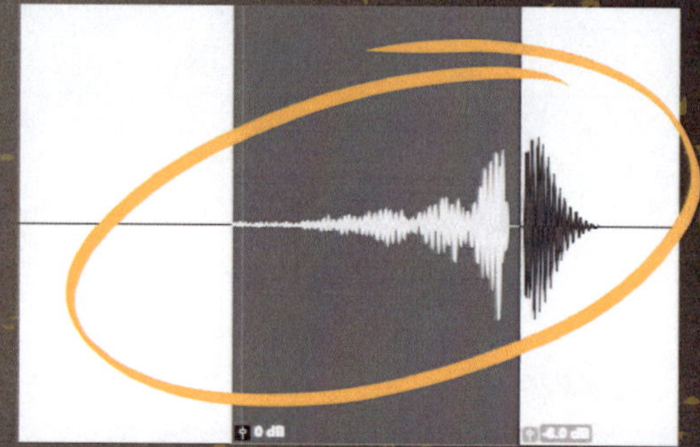

6 Apply fades and enjoy your reverse effect...

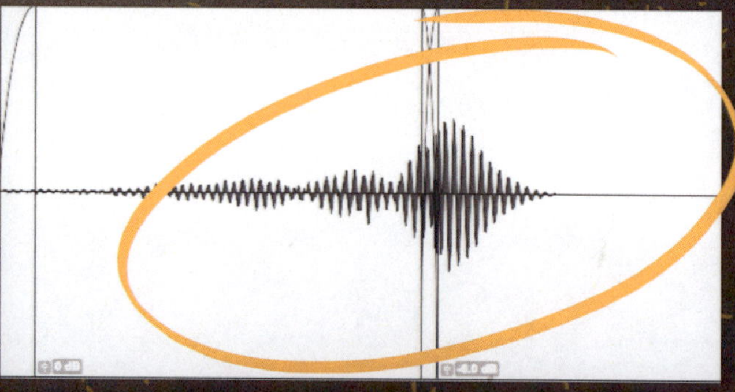

The Classic Vinyl Record Stop Trick!

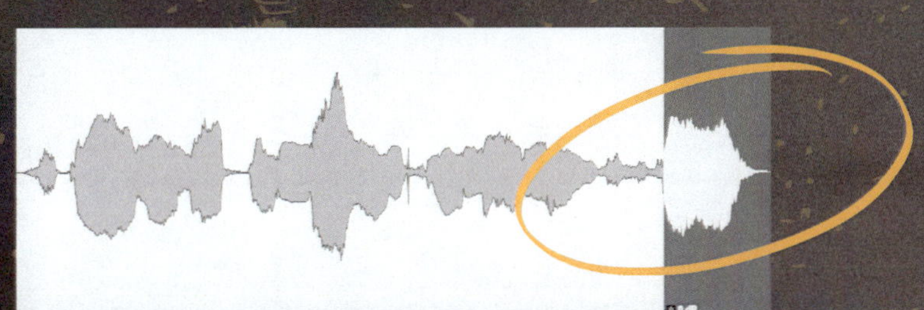

1 Select the last word or piece of sound in a phrase...

2 Choose the Vari-Fi AudioSuite...

3 Select the "Slow Down" feature...

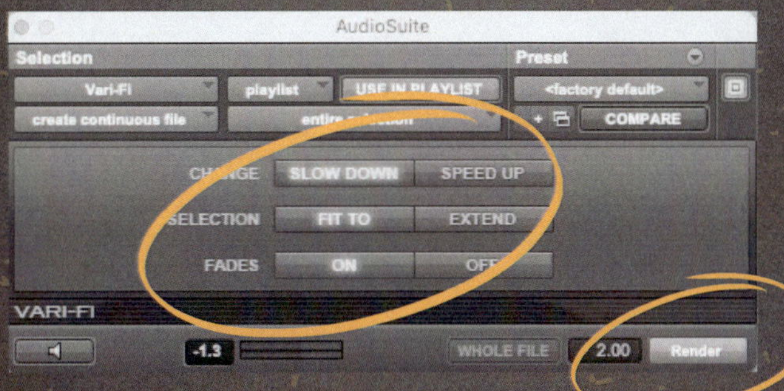

4 Render the Vari-Fi effect...

5 Notice the waveform change and enjoy the Vinyl Record Stop Trick!

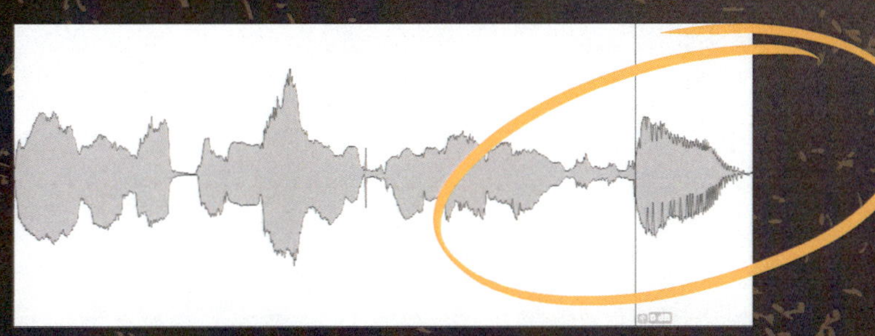

The Human Ear
(Fletcher Munson Curve)

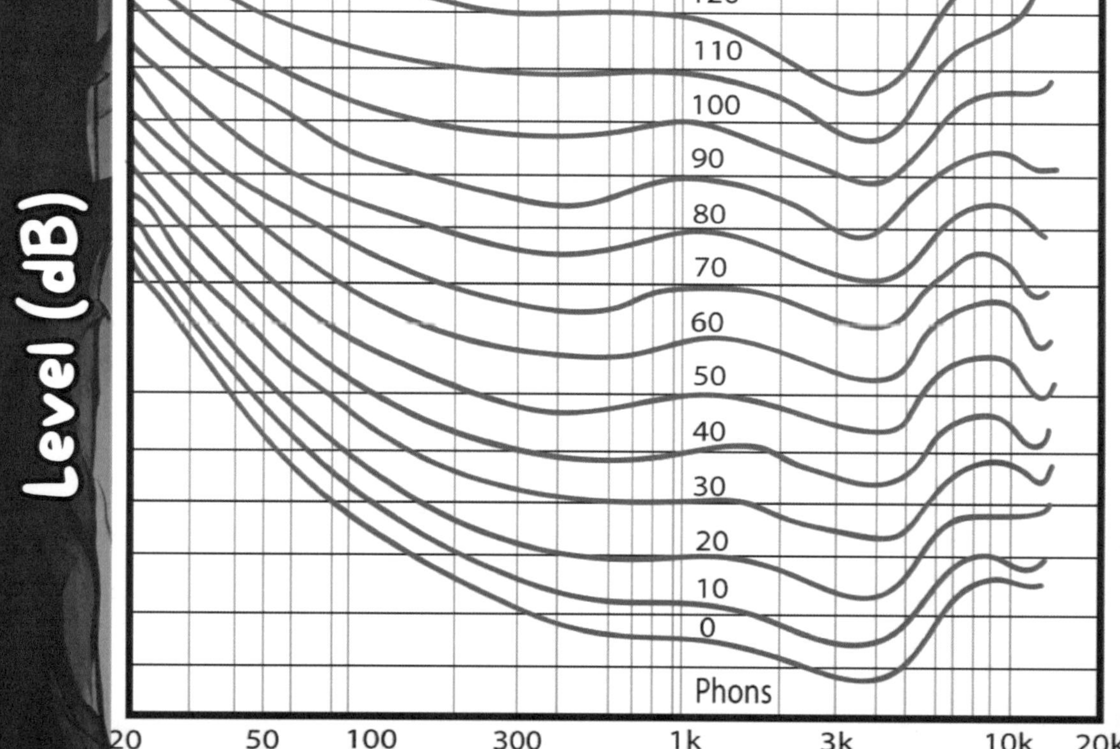

Humans perceive the frequency spectrum differently depending on the volume level. Additionally, varying volumes are required at different frequencies for us to perceive the spectrum as balanced. Notice the volume dip between 2k-6k and the amplified volume at the lower and higher ends of the spectrum. This occurs because humans are most sensitive to upper mid frequencies, and we need more volume to perceive the outermost frequencies in the spectrum. Additionally, the most accurate or neutral representation of the spectrum is typically perceived at approximately 85dB.
(This is the ideal volume for mixing)

Higher Frequency Reference Points

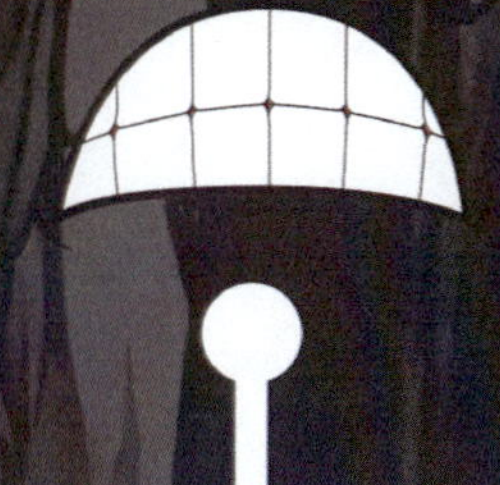

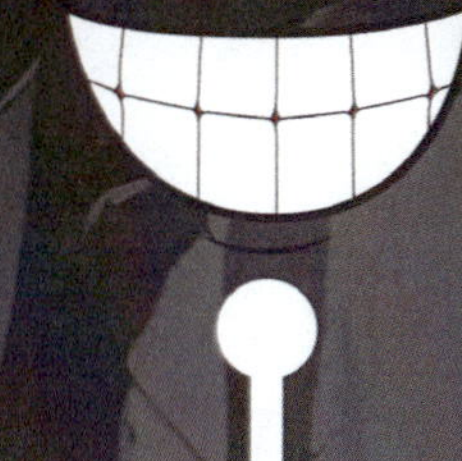

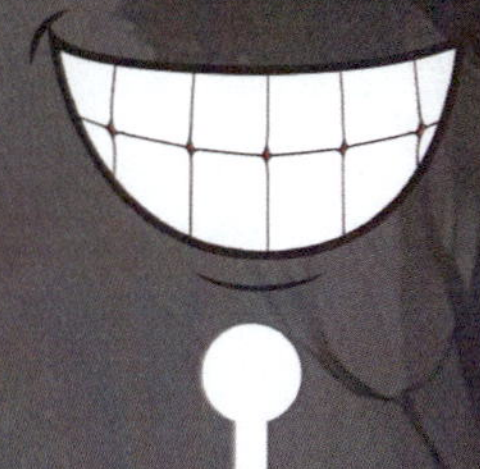

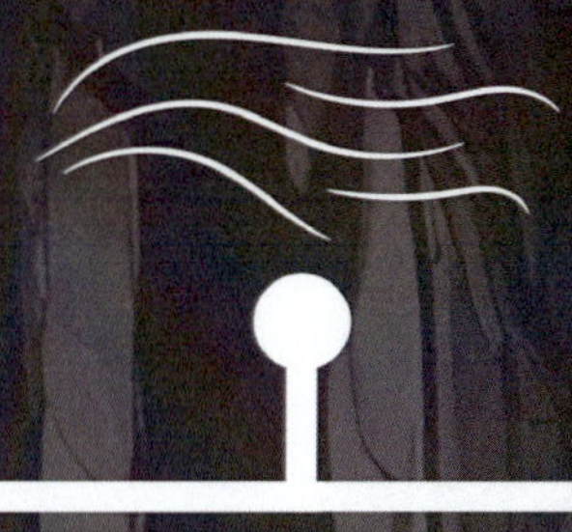

Low Teeth "Sh" — 4-6 kHz

Too much
4-6 kHz can be harsh on the ears. Transient details are frequently found in this frequency range.

Not enough
4-6 kHz can lead to a lack of energy, resulting in a dull sound.

Teeth "Ss" — 6-12 kHz

Too much
6-12 kHz may result in excessive sibilance and a lack of smoothness.

Not enough
6-12 kHz can lead to a lack of clarity and articulation.

Tip of the Teeth "Sss!" — 12-16 kHz

Too much
12-16 kHz can take on a "hissing" quality which over time can lead to ear fatigue.

Not enough
12-16 kHz can cause a lack of brightness, resulting in the ear perceiving a "muddy" sound.

Air "Hhh" — 16-20 kHz

Too much
16-20 kHz can create a tiring atmosphere that can eventually causes ear fatigue.

Not enough
16-20 kHz can lead to a diminished sense of "openness" and cause the ear to focus more on lower, harsher frequencies.

Midrange Frequency Reference Points

Low "Howl"	Low Comfortable "Whistle"	High Comfortable "Whistle"	High "Whistle"
	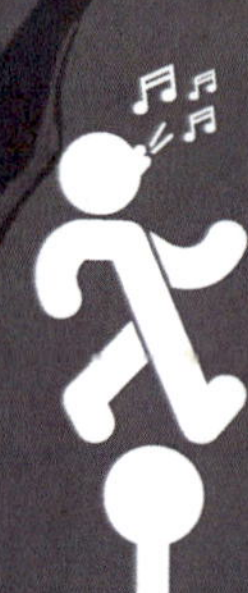		
400-800 Hz	800 Hz – 1 kHz	1-2 kHz	2-4 kHz

Too much 400-800 Hz can result in a "Cloudy" or "Howling" midrange.

Not enough 400-800 Hz can lead the ear to hear resonances in the surrounding midrange frequencies.

Too much 800 Hz – 1 kHz can create "Papery" or "Hollow" resonance in the midrange.

Not enough 800 Hz – 1 kHz will create a lack of midrange harmonics that are fundamental for many instruments and voices.

Too much 1-2 kHz can lead to an unpleasant "Ambient" or "Whistling" resonance, which may be harsh on the ears.

Not enough 1-2 kHz can lead to a lack of intelligibility in sounds such dialogue.

Too much 2-4 kHz can cause an unpleasant "Biting" harshness that triggers the sensitive range of human hearing.

Not enough 2-4 kHz may result in a lack of articulation or "punch" in the sound.

Lower Frequency Reference Points

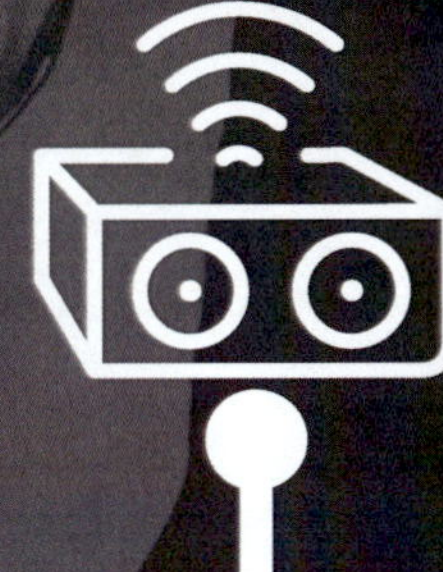

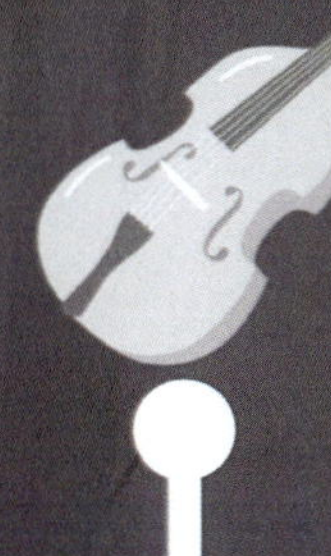

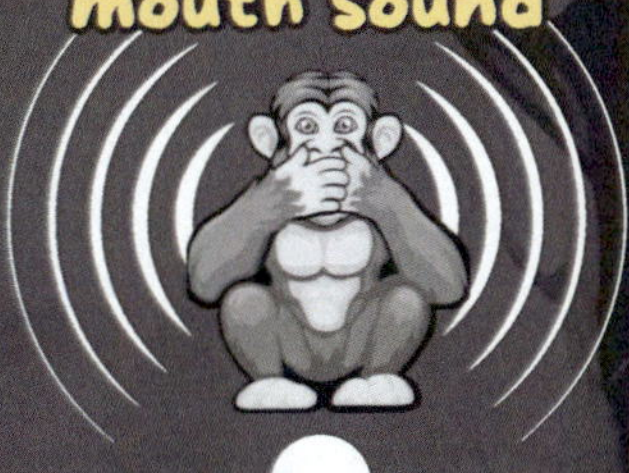

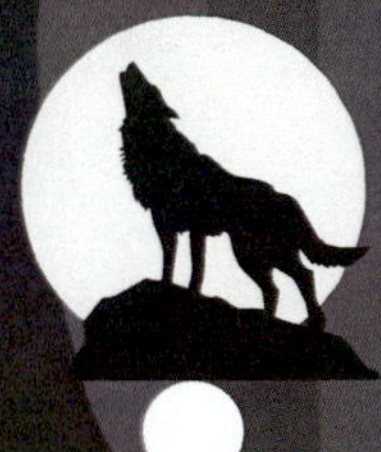

20-60 Hz

60-150 Hz

150-300 Hz

300-400 Hz

Too much
20-60 Hz can overwhelm the clarity of the overall frequency spectrum. It can also potentially lead to negative physical responses.

Not enough
20-60 Hz can shift the ear's attention from the low end to the lower mid range, creating an underwhelming experience.

Too much
60-150 Hz can create a sense of "boominess" that can overpower a mix.

Not enough
60-150 can result in a "thin" sound that lacks low end "punch". This can also result in a "mid-rangy" sound.

Too much
150-300 Hz can create a sense of "muffling" or "muddiness" that fights clarity in the sound.

Not enough
150-300 Hz may lack "warmth," leading to a "thin" sound.

Too much
300-400 Hz may lead to a "howling" effect, diminishing definition in other frequency ranges.

Not enough
300-400 Hz can create a "scooped" mid-range effect, exaggerating the "boominess" and "harshness" in a mix.

Technical Proficiency

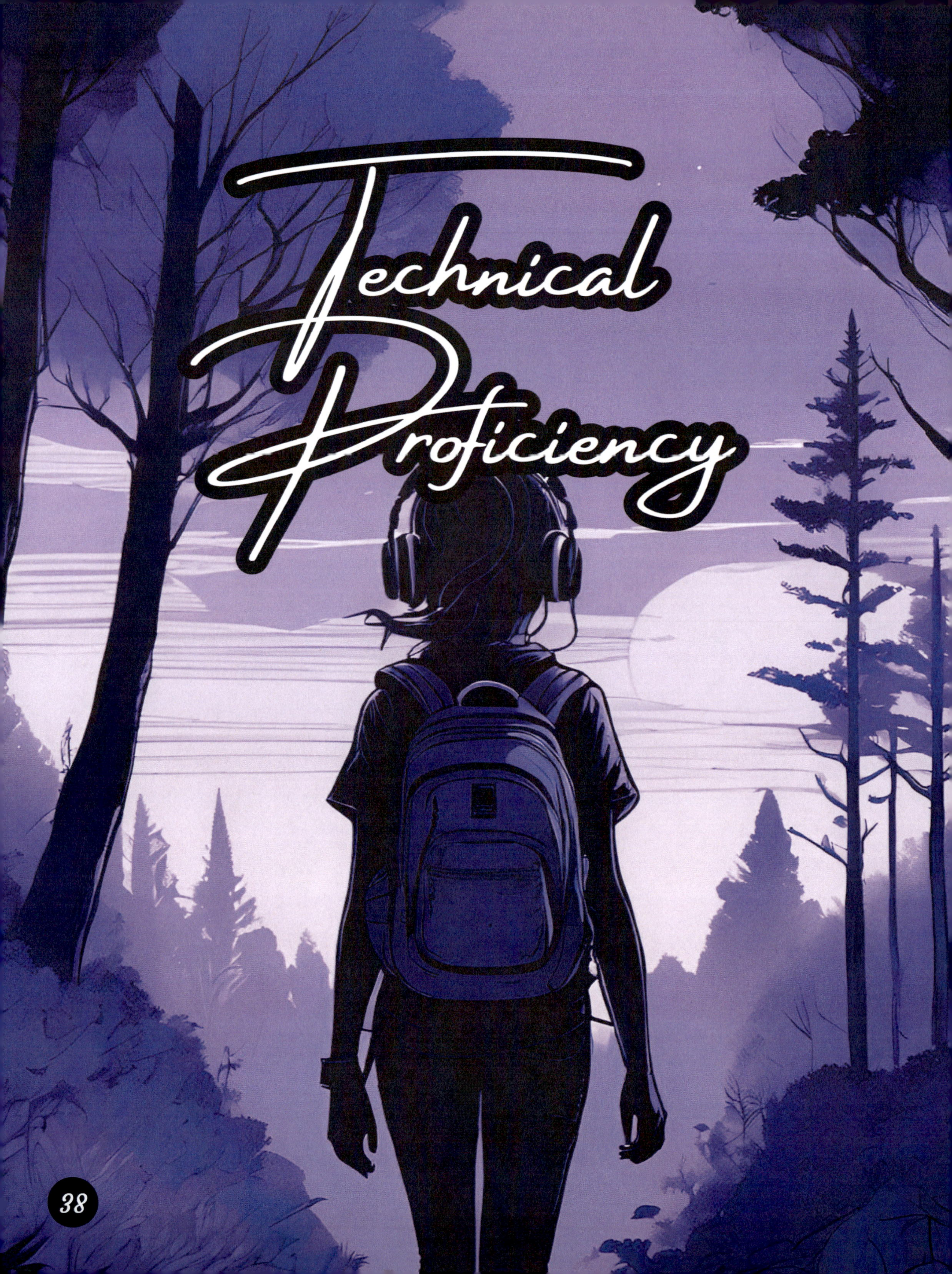

What is Signal Flow?

Signal flow is the journey in which an audio signal travels...

The technical proficiency of an audio engineer relies significantly on their ability to manage audio routing and follow signal flow.

Mixing Console Basic Concept

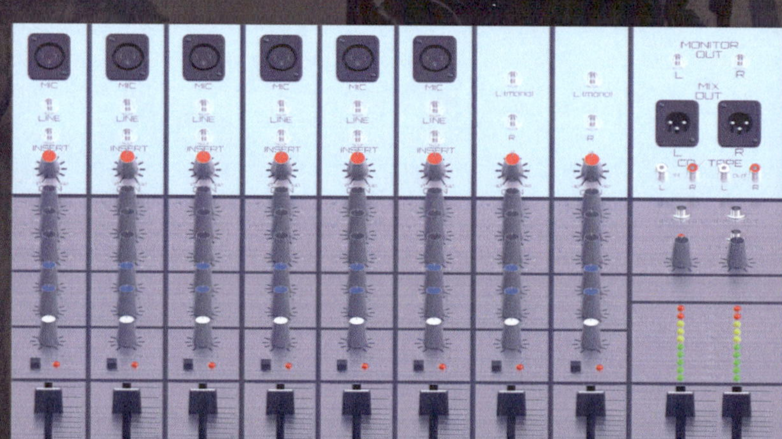

Physical Input

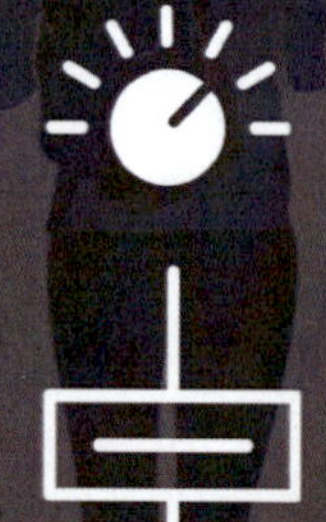
Input Channel

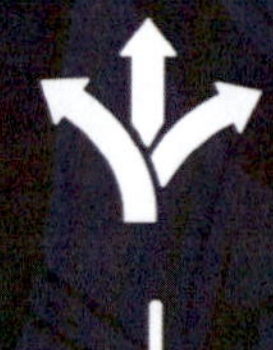
Mix Bus

Physical Output

Physical Input

Direct Signal

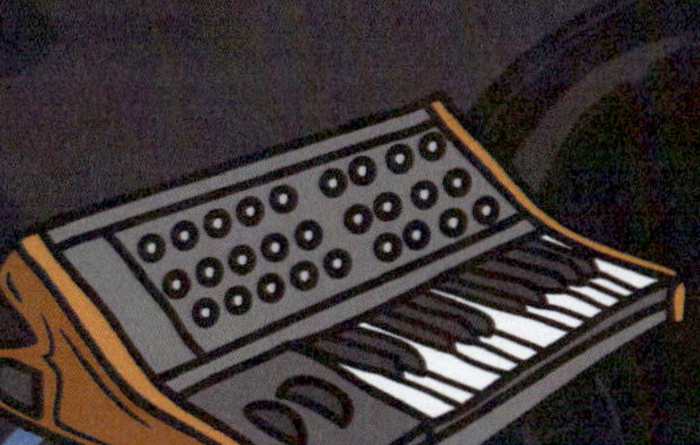

Mic Signal

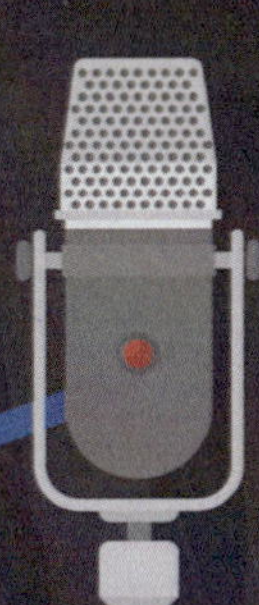

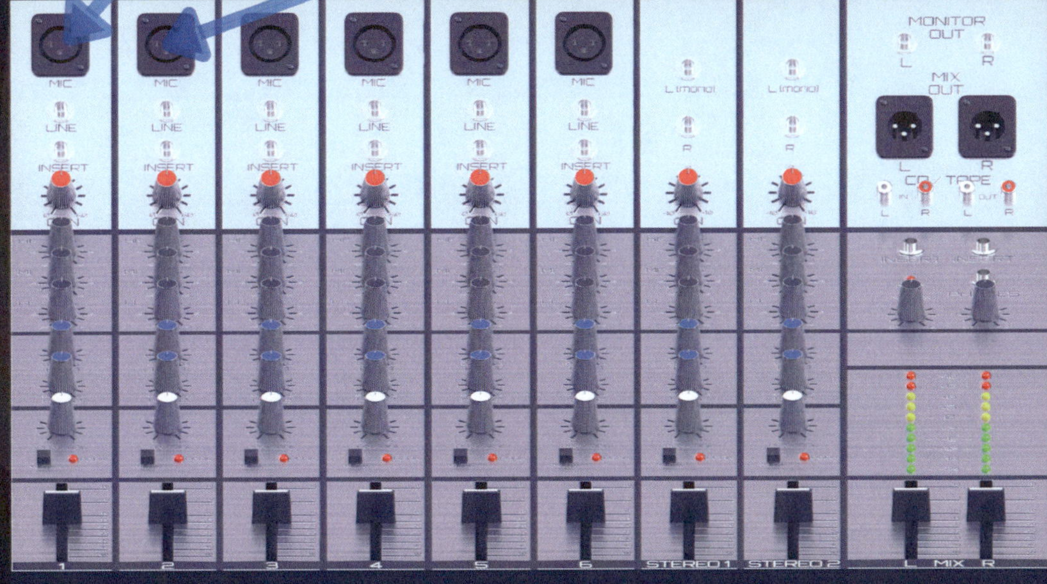

*The physical location audio enters a piece of gear.....

Input Channel
"The Channel Strip"

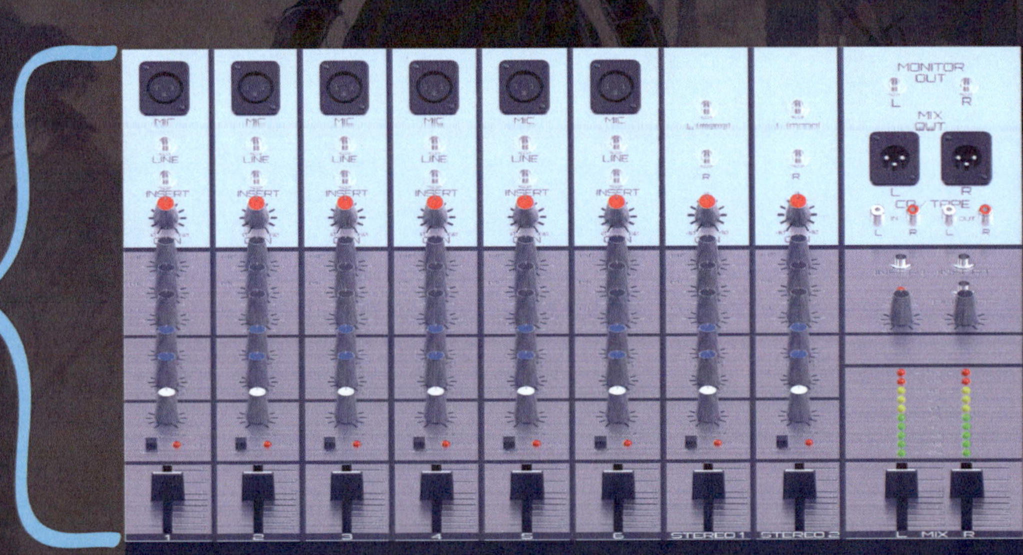

Microphone
Pre-Amplifier
"Mic Pre"

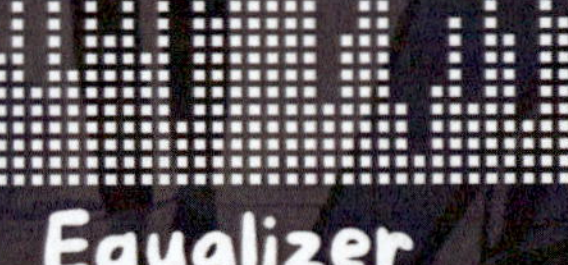

Equalizer
"EQ"

Dynamics
"Compression/Gate"

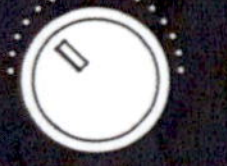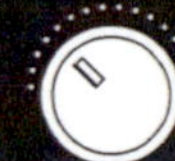

Auxiliary and
FX Sends
"Sends"

Input Chanel
Fader

Physical Output

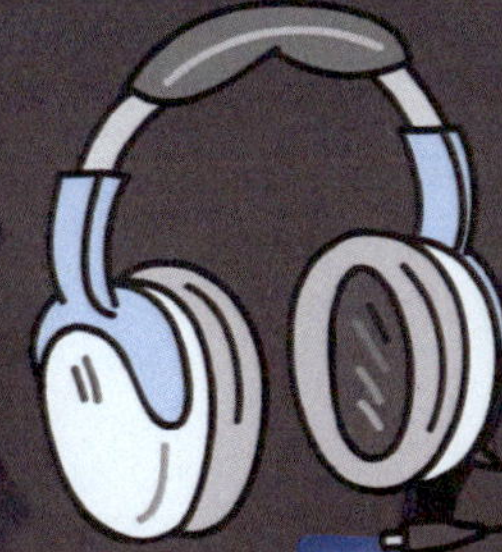

Headphones

Speakers

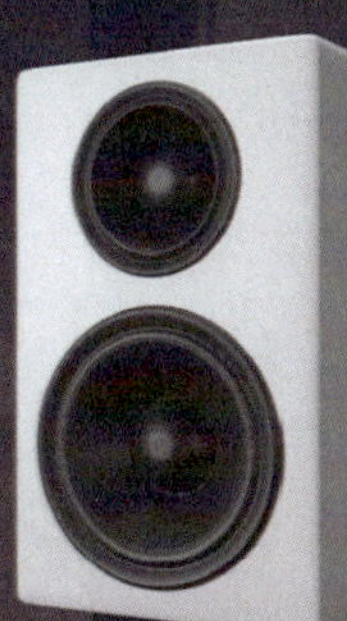

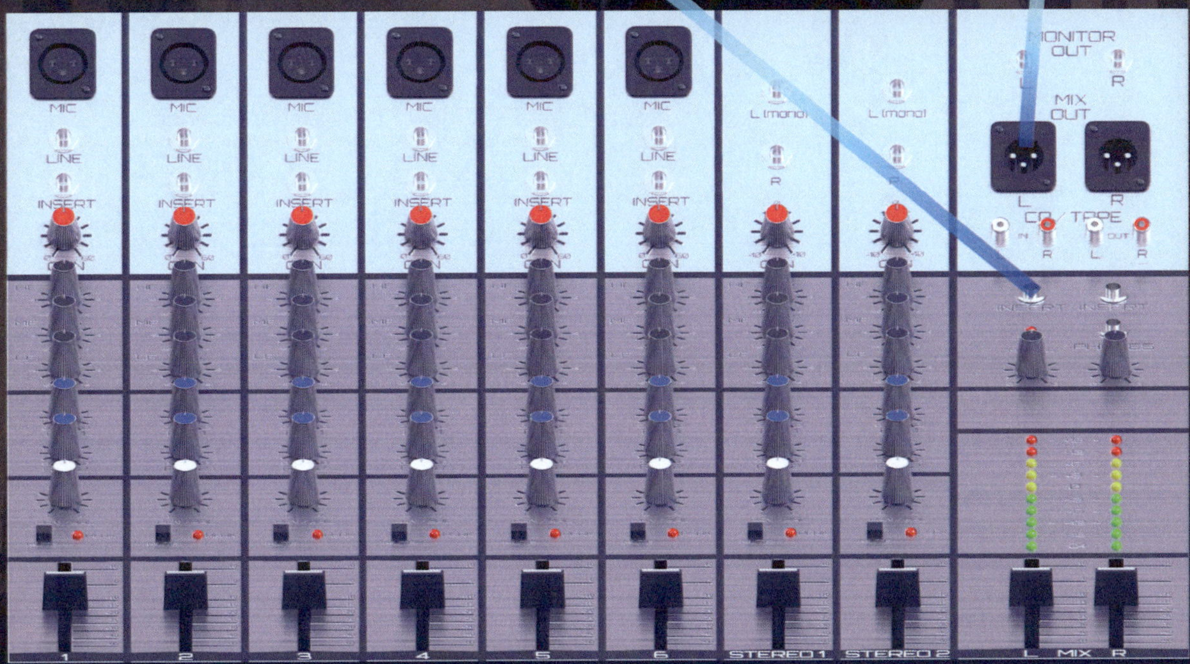

*The physical location audio exits
a piece of gear.....

The Mixbus Hierarchy

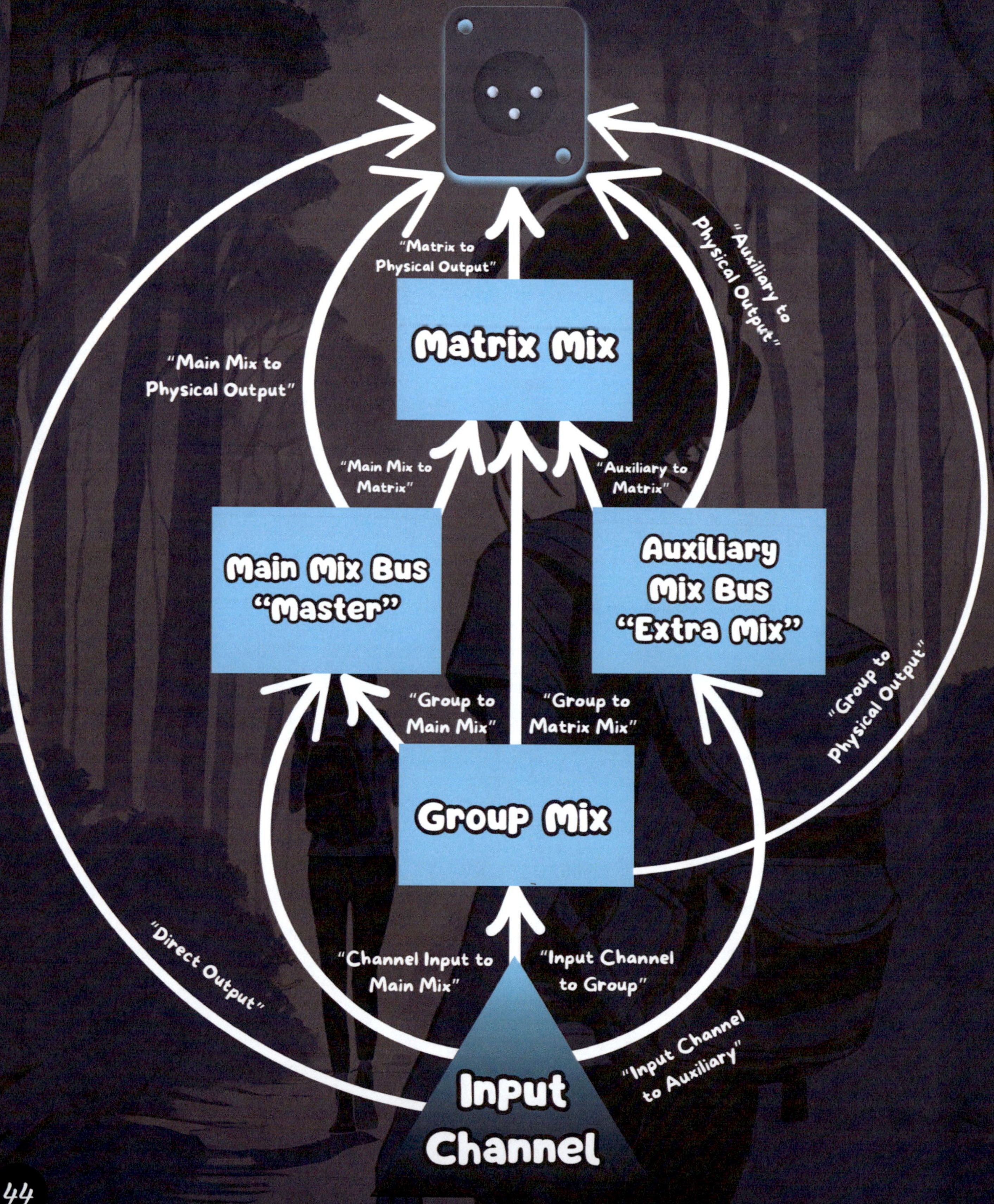

What is Gain Staging?

Gain Staging is the act of optimizing audio signal levels by achieving the best signal to noise ratio, while demonstrating relative fader position to what you hear...

Much like a doctor practices medicine....
An audio engineer practices gain staging...

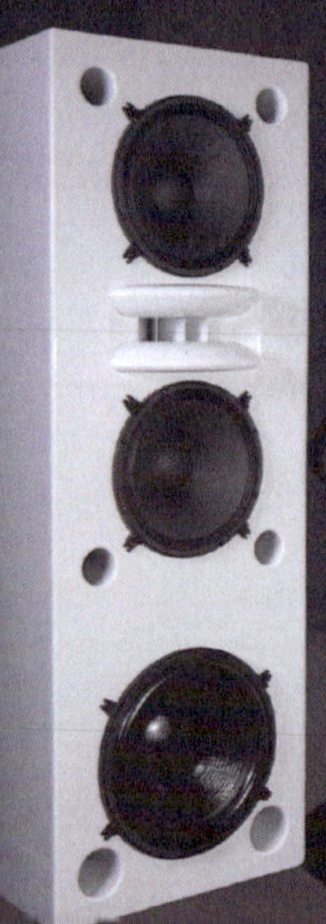
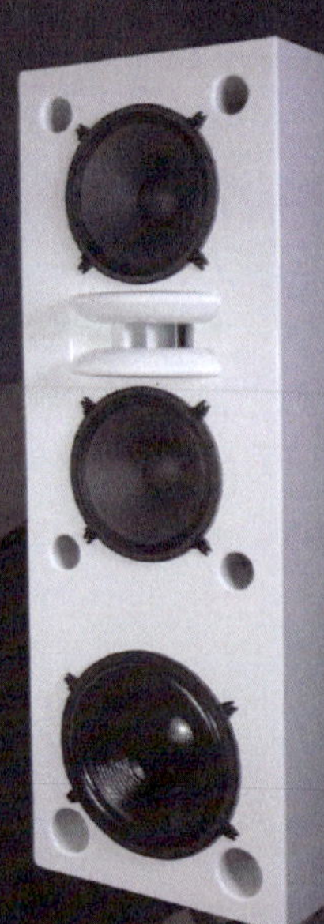

Speaker Level: The output level of the speaker amplifier

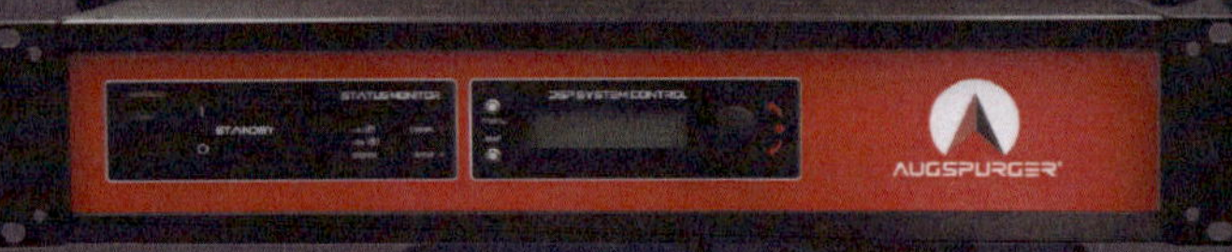

Speaker Amplifier

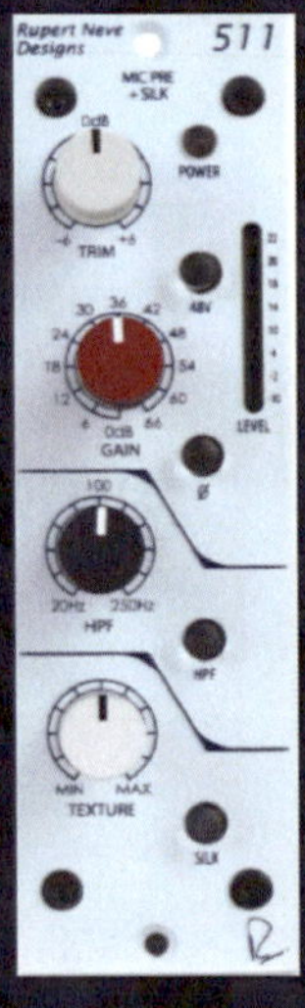

Microphone Pre-Amplifier

Line Level: The output level of a pre-amp and mixing console

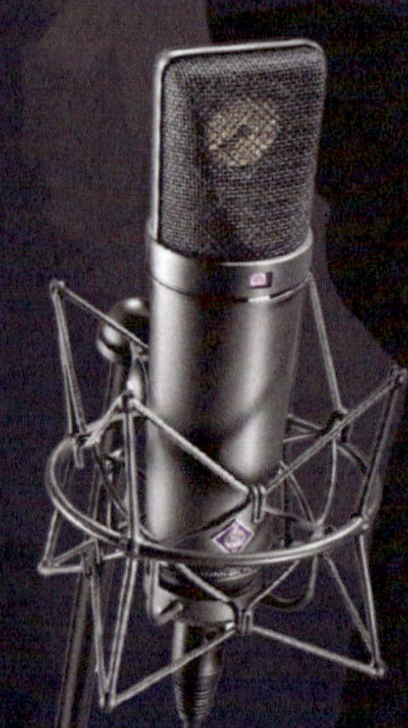

Mic Level: The output level of a microphone

Preamp Technique

Start with the "Trim" or "Output" at Unity (0dB)...

Try some different flavors...

Raise the "Gain" until the signal is reading between -18dB and -12dB on your DAW input...

Boost the "Gain and reduce the "Trim" to enhance saturation.

Reduce the "Gain and boost the "Trim" for a cleaner sound.

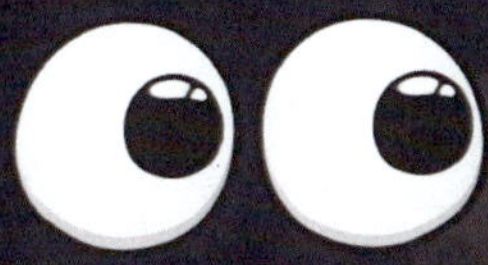

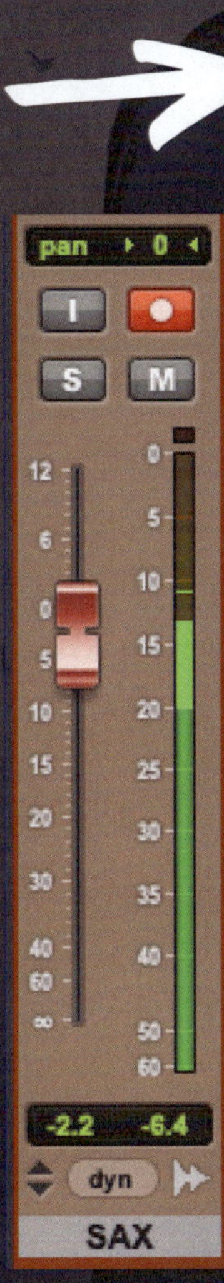

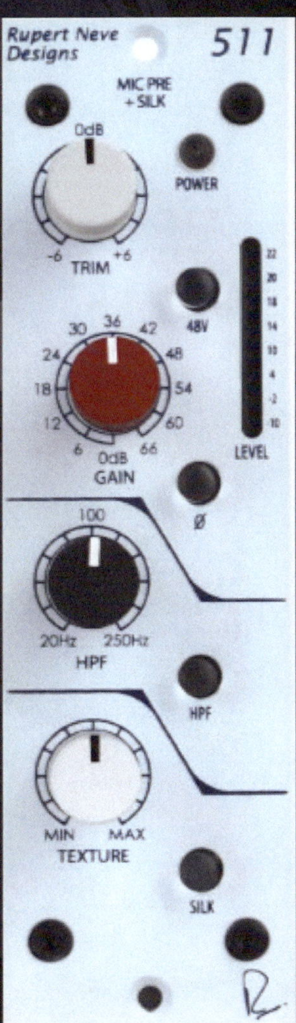

Recording Levels

Turning up a weak signal will amplify and expose the noise floor.

Turning down a distorted signal won't get rid of the distrotion.

This balance is ideal! You can tweak this signal up or down without any negative consequences.

Recording a signal with too weak of a signal will result in a noisy signal.

Recording a signal too strong can result in a distorted signal.

Recording a signal at the same level as your desired output will result in the best signal to noise ratio.

Relative Fader Position

At the end of the day, the "sound" is what matter most. However, it's important to prepare your "gain structure" in a way that creates an intuitive workflow. This will make balancing and distributing mixes a much easier and efficient process. The relationship between how signal strength looks and the volume that is perceived by a listener can be quite misleading. This is do to the speed in which various types of meters react to transients, as well as how our ears perceive volume at particular frequencies.

By first setting the faders in a position "relative" to the balance you want to hear, you can then balance the mix at the "pre-amp level" (setting the gain structure for everything in the mixer). This does not mean "Don't touch your faders!". Remember this is a technique for calibrating your gain structure, not the mix itself. Avoid losing sleep over perfect gain structure, as sound and music is a moving target. After all, you can always "re-gain structure" if you find yourself fighting your faders, overdriving a channel, or capturing a noisy weak signal. Remember, this is a practice, much like how a doctor practices medicine, an engineer practices gain structure.

1

Turn both the pre-amp and speaker levels and all the way down..

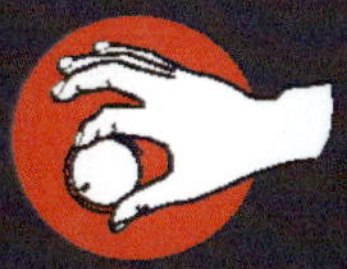

2

Raise your master fader to unity and your input faders to a uniform level (either unity or -5dB)

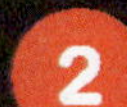
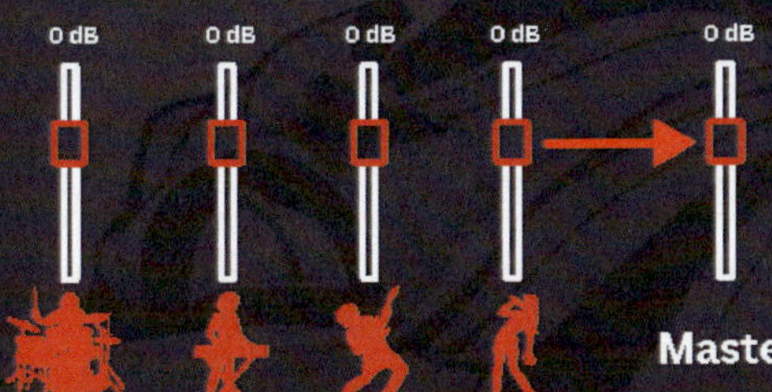

3

Increase the pre-amp gain for either the vocal or kick drum until your input signal reaches around -12dB to -8dB at its loudest points. This will leave you headroom in case the artist gets excited during their performance....

These tracks tend to meter a little higher than other instruments, making them a great signal reference for setting your speaker volume in the next step...

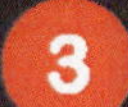

4

Determine your listening level by turn up the speakers until your "kick drum" feels appropriately loud for the situation...

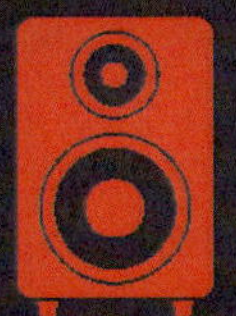
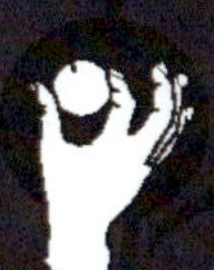
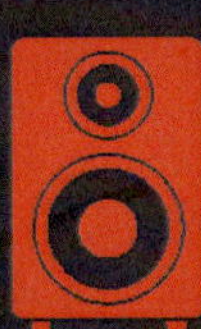

5

Now since you have established the appropriate volume for your speakers, balance the remaining inputs using only pre-amps to establish a basic mix...

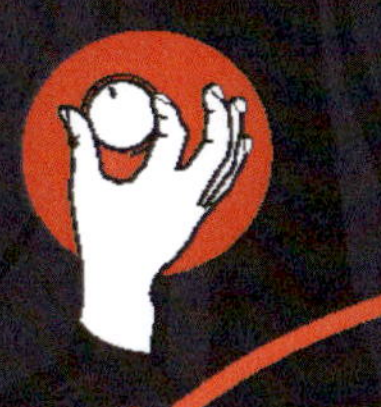

6

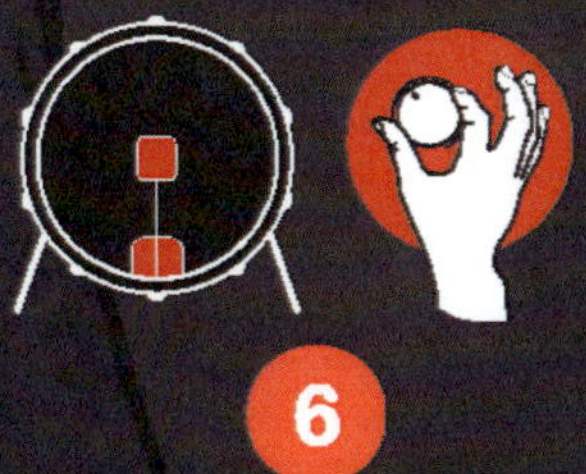

If you have done all 5 steps, you will realize the mix "sounds" balanced with faders in a uniform position... Now your fader movements will show "relativity" to the mix you are hearing. Notice the "relative fader position" demonstrated with these mixes below.

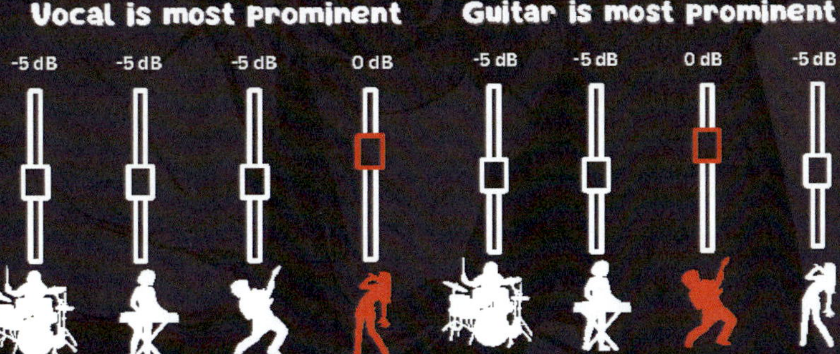

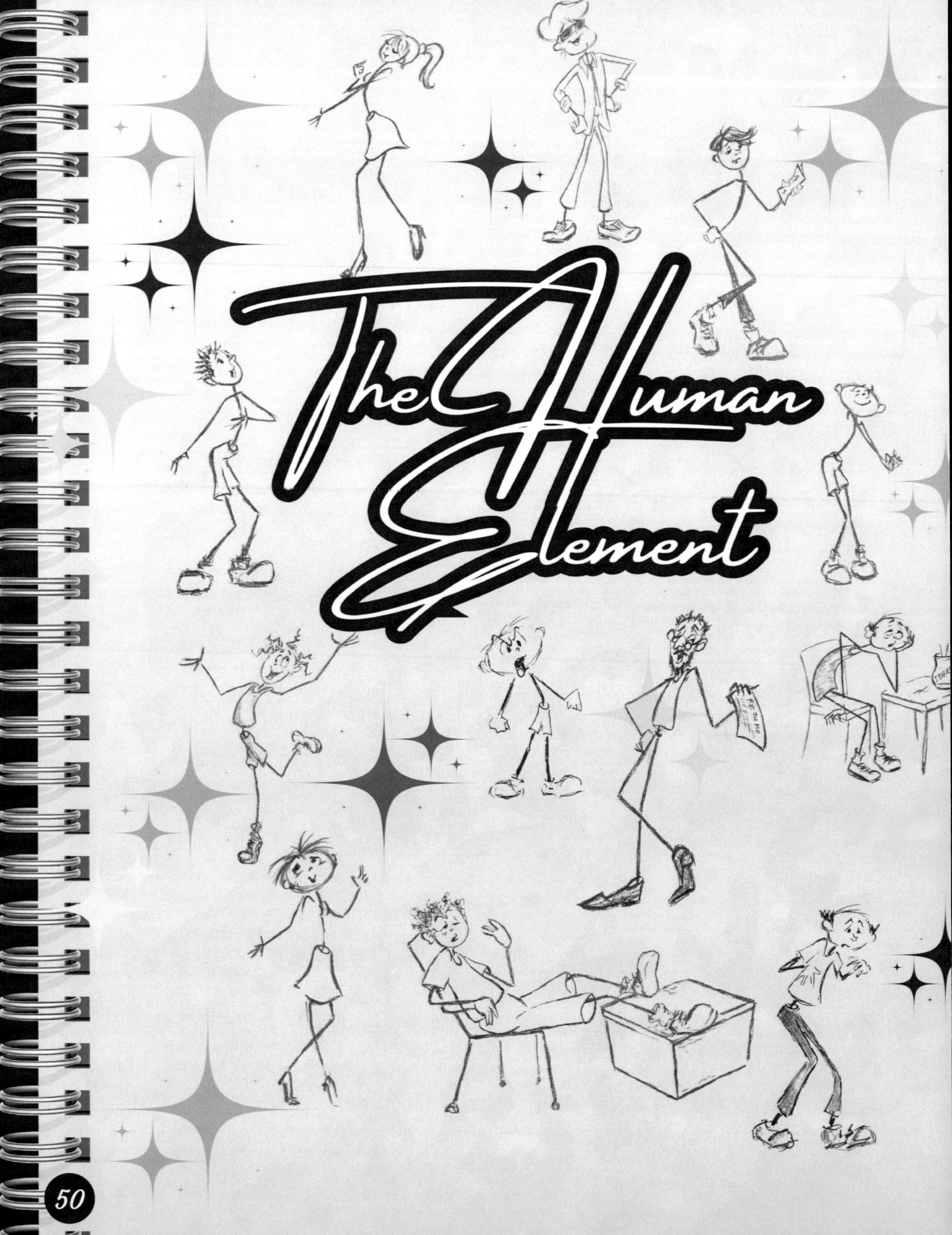

The Human Element

Judgment in the Pendulum Process!

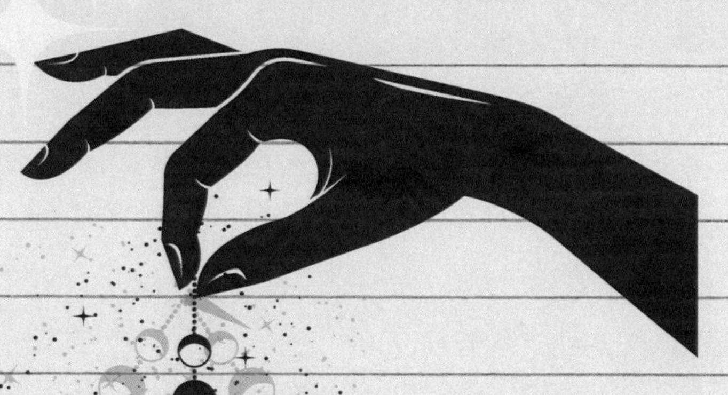

Logically Correct Decision

Socially Appropriate Decision

Tasteful Decision

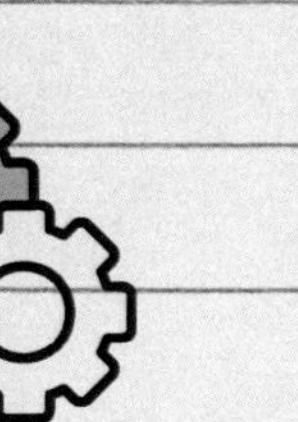

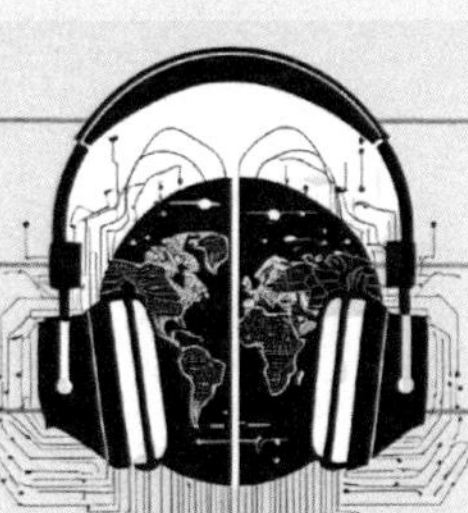

Pro: Can resolve a tangible problem...

Con: Can lack inspiration and sometimes come across cold at heart...

Pro: Can resolve social conflict...

Con: Can leave a tangible problem unresolved, resulting in goal shortcomings...

Hosting the Session

To ensure a seamless session, give yourself extra time to focus on the subtle details that significantly enhance the production experience. As the host of a recording session or production meeting, your objective is to foster a safe and comfortable environment for all participants. This involves preparing a checklist of necessary technical elements and hospitality considerations. Artists appreciate the thoughtful touches that show you are there to support them. This could include providing tea, water, a notepad for lyrics, or even creating an inviting atmosphere with mood lighting and candles.

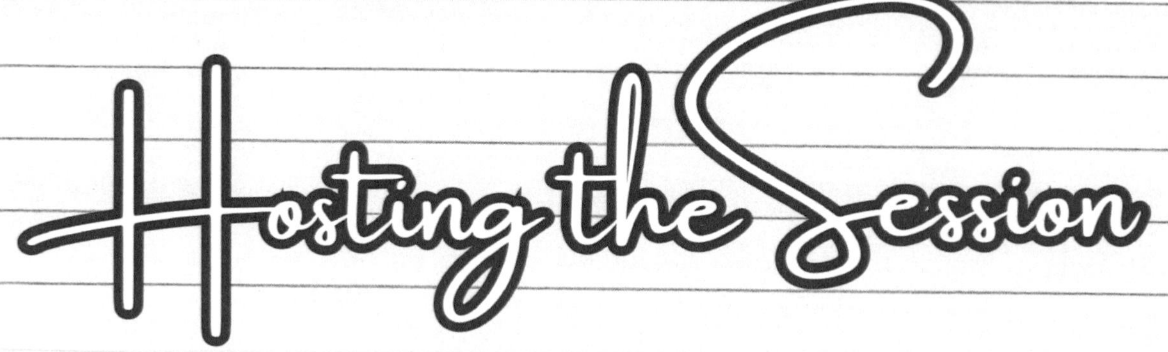

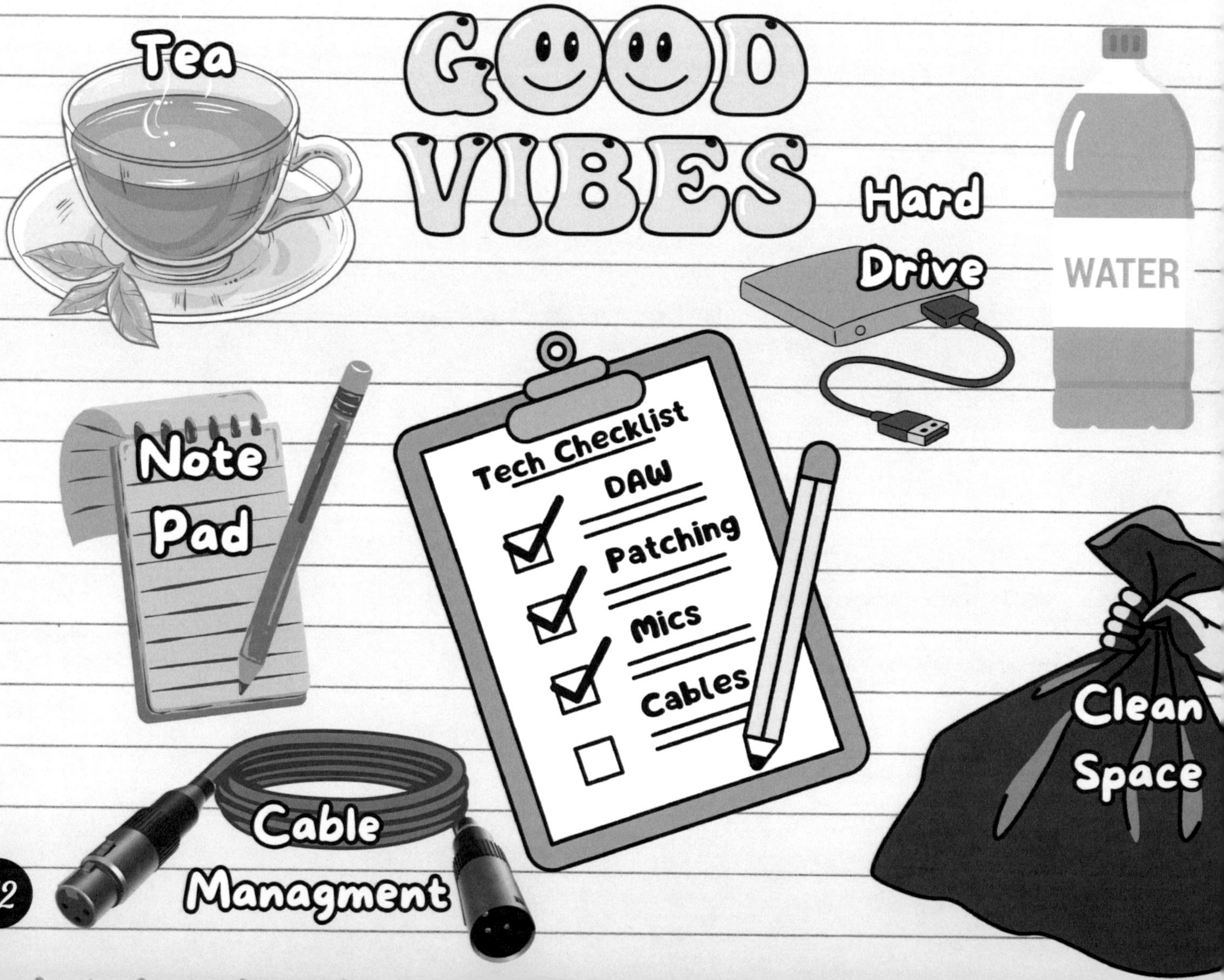

Hosting the Party

From the engineer's perspective, conducting a recording session is a lot like hosting a party...

As you continue to become more comfortable with your technical and artistic abilities, be sure to develop your hospitality skills...

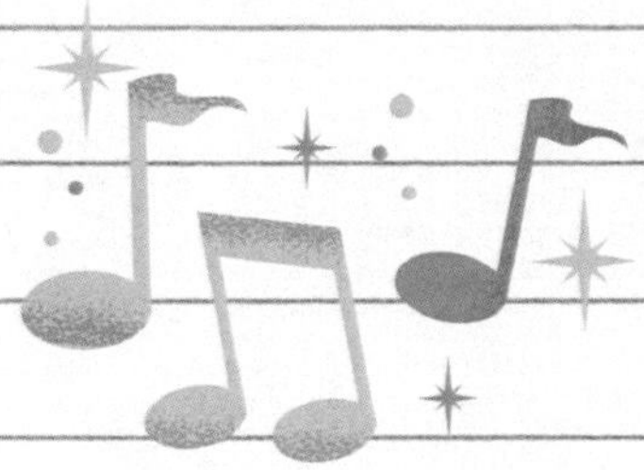

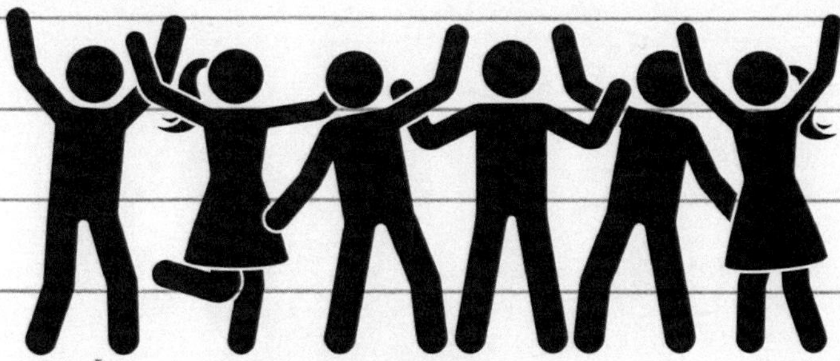

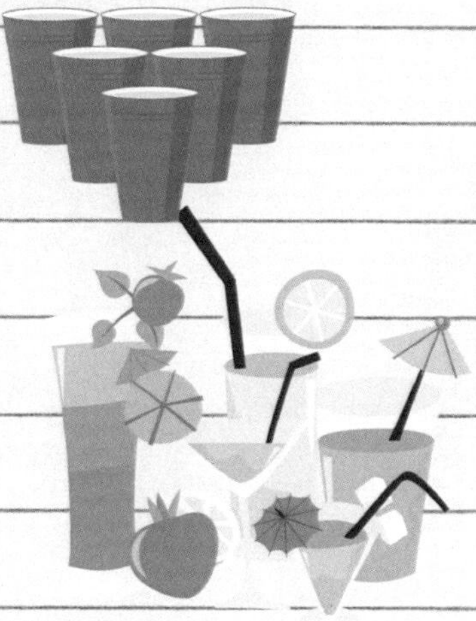

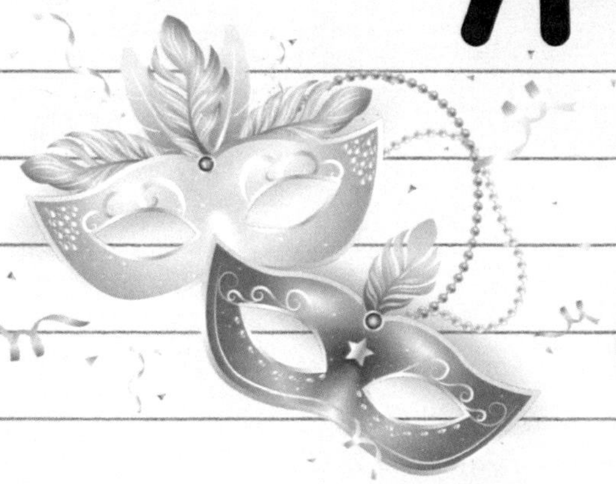

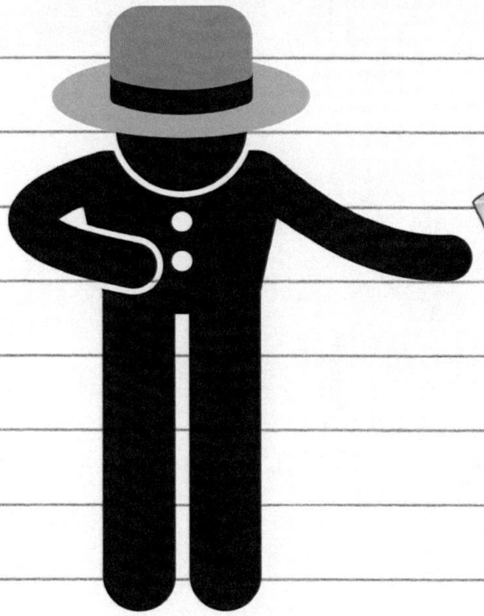

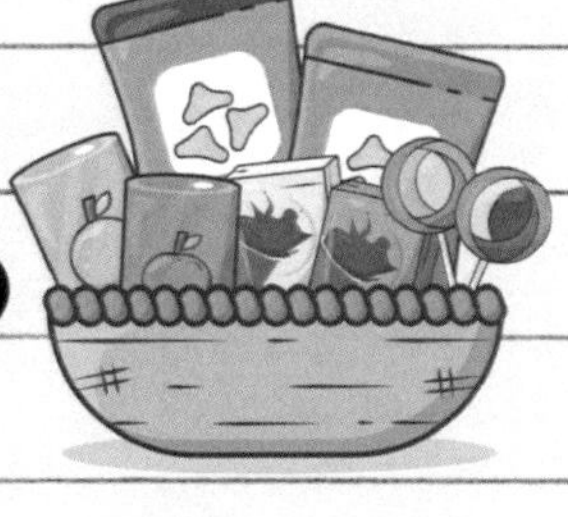

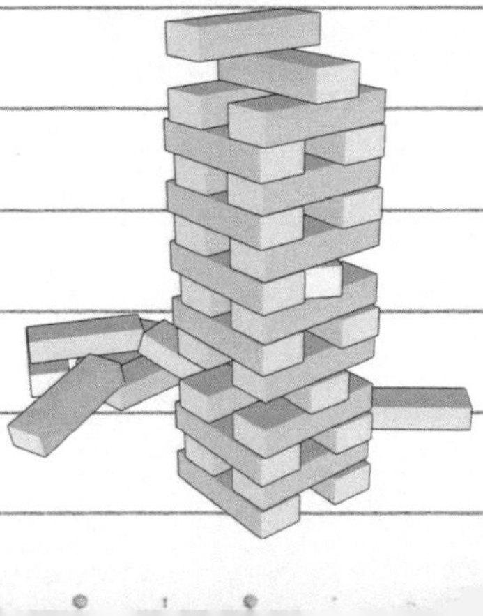

Personality Types

You are about to meet various personality types that are commonly found in a production environment. Although many of these characters may remind you of someone you know, elements of each of these personalities may exist within you as well. Rather than labeling them as merely good or bad, strive to empathize with each personality and discover ways to maintain productivity despite these differences. Keep in mind that you cannot change others, but you can develop a flexible understanding of them. In a professional setting, not everyone can be your best friend, but a mutual understanding is essential for both the project and your mental wellbeing.

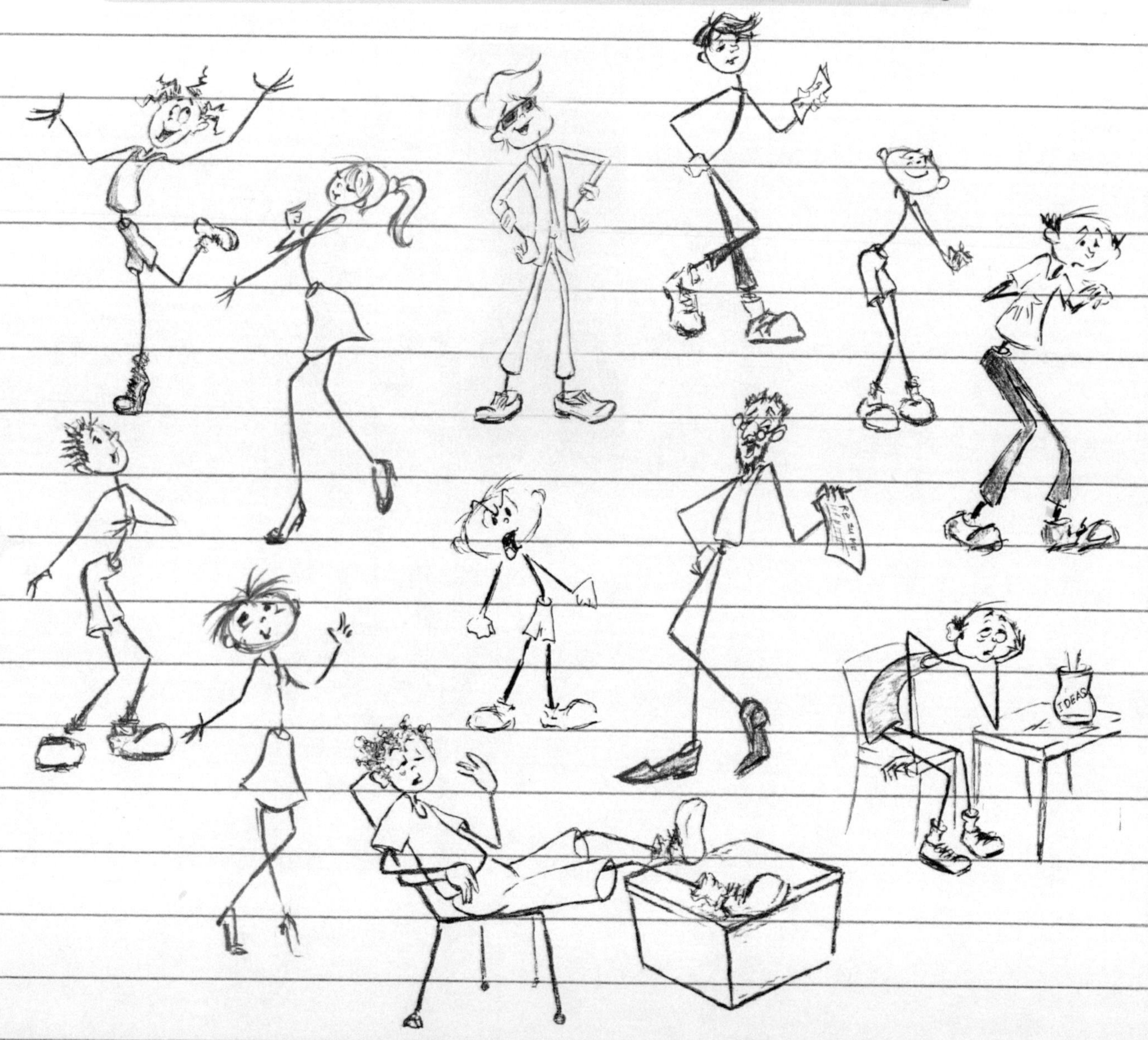

Joey "Bighead"

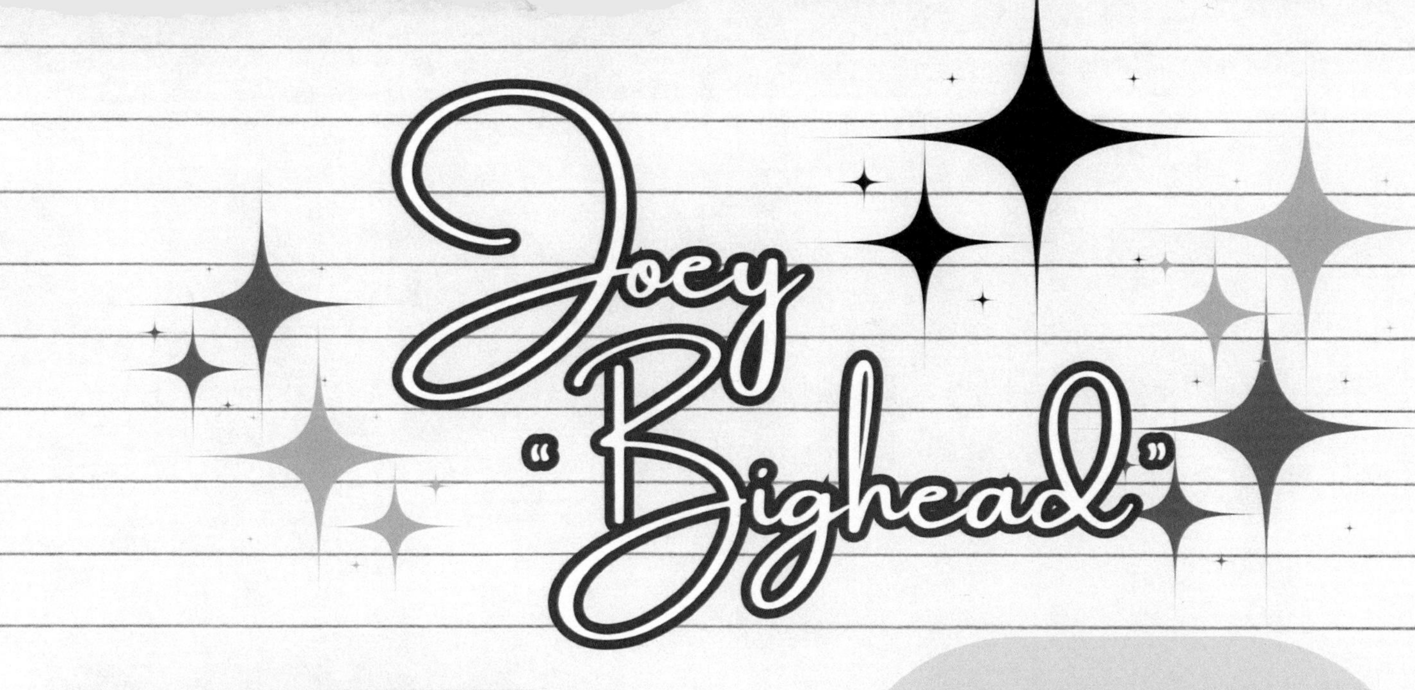

Joey is the charismatic and talented person in the group. He plays an essential role within the team, though he does have a fairly large ego. His presence often generates considerable social pressure among others. If you encounter Joey don't be afraid to express your thoughts, but be careful not to deflate his ego. Remember, allow him to feel special as confidence is crucial in difficult situations.

Gabby "Group Think"

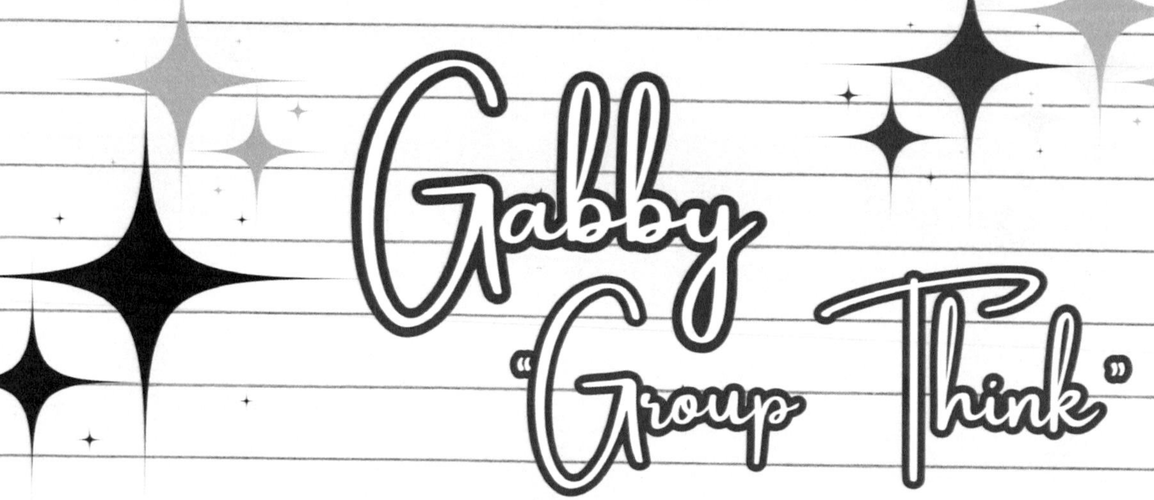

Group Think:

the social pressure within a group to conform to a popular belief. These decisions often conflict with logic and can severely hinder a group's success.

This scenario serves as a clear illustration of group think. It's often the case that newer or younger members within a group experience high social pressure. Perhaps her role in the situation would make it inappropriate to share a bold opinion. In this moment, it's vital for Gabby to make a tasteful choice in balancing a logical decision vs. a socially appropriate decision. While it's natural to want to be accepted within a group, it's essential to recognize that one of the most significant obstacles to a project's success is the social dynamics tied to group think.

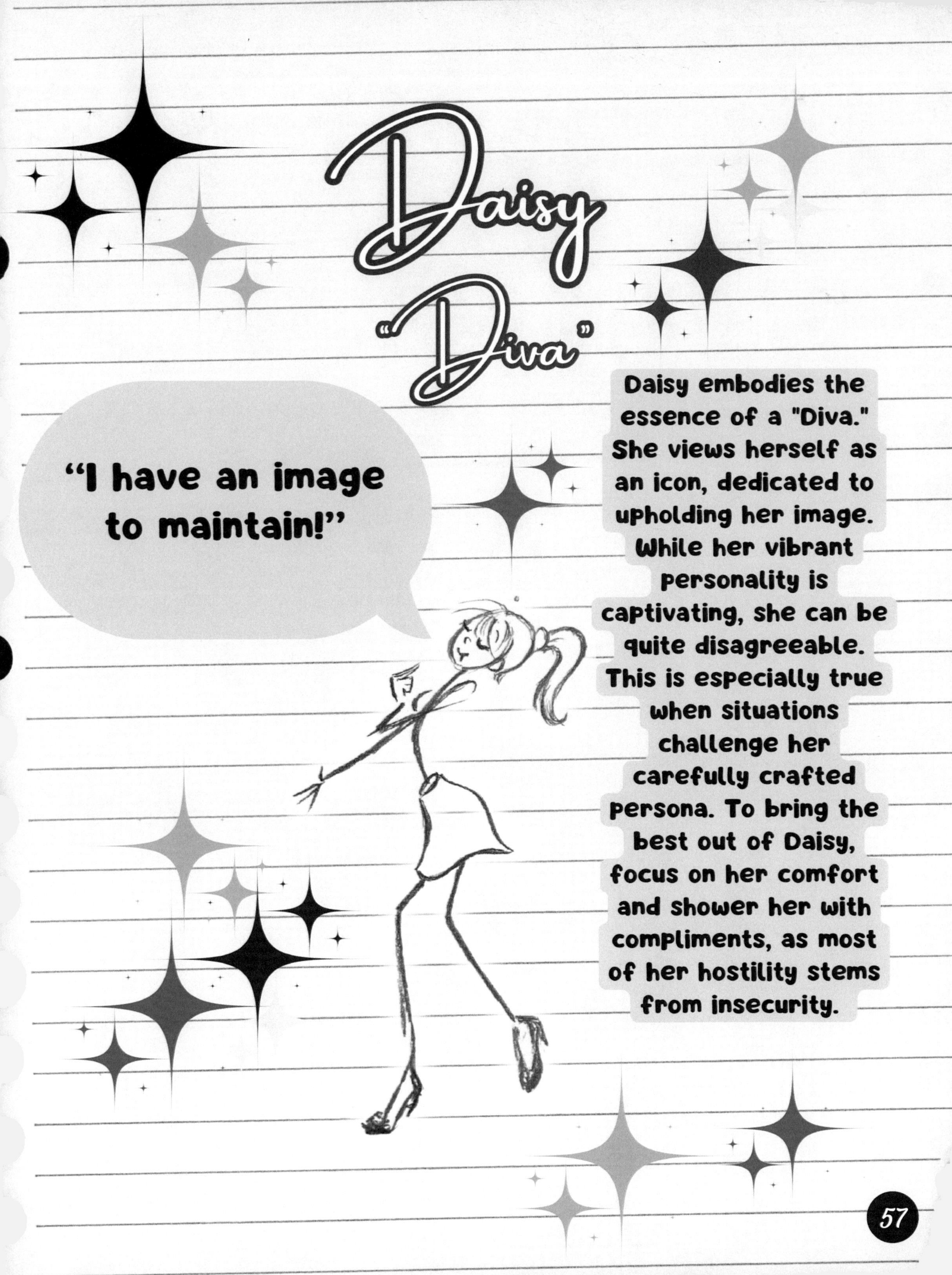

Daisy embodies the essence of a "Diva." She views herself as an icon, dedicated to upholding her image. While her vibrant personality is captivating, she can be quite disagreeable. This is especially true when situations challenge her carefully crafted persona. To bring the best out of Daisy, focus on her comfort and shower her with compliments, as most of her hostility stems from insecurity.

"Got a Crush" Carl

Carl embodies the well-known struggle between personal and professional boundaries. His affection for the lovely Daisy often clouds his judgment, leading to biased decisions in her favor. While things may appear fine initially, complications often emerge when disagreements arise between Daisy and Carl. Their capacity for constructive criticism diminishes, while emotional tensions escalate. In essence, resolving issues becomes increasingly complex due to the increased emotional factor.

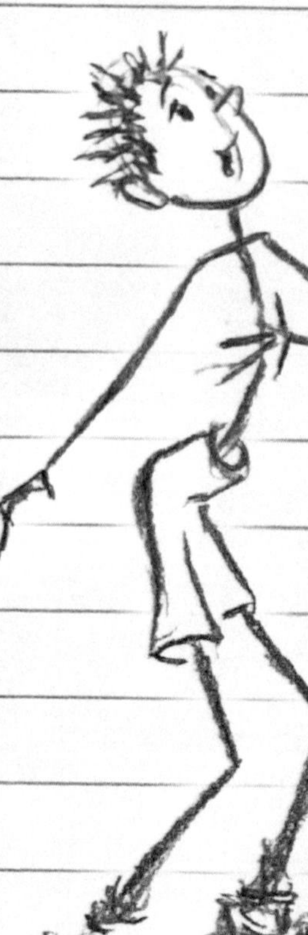

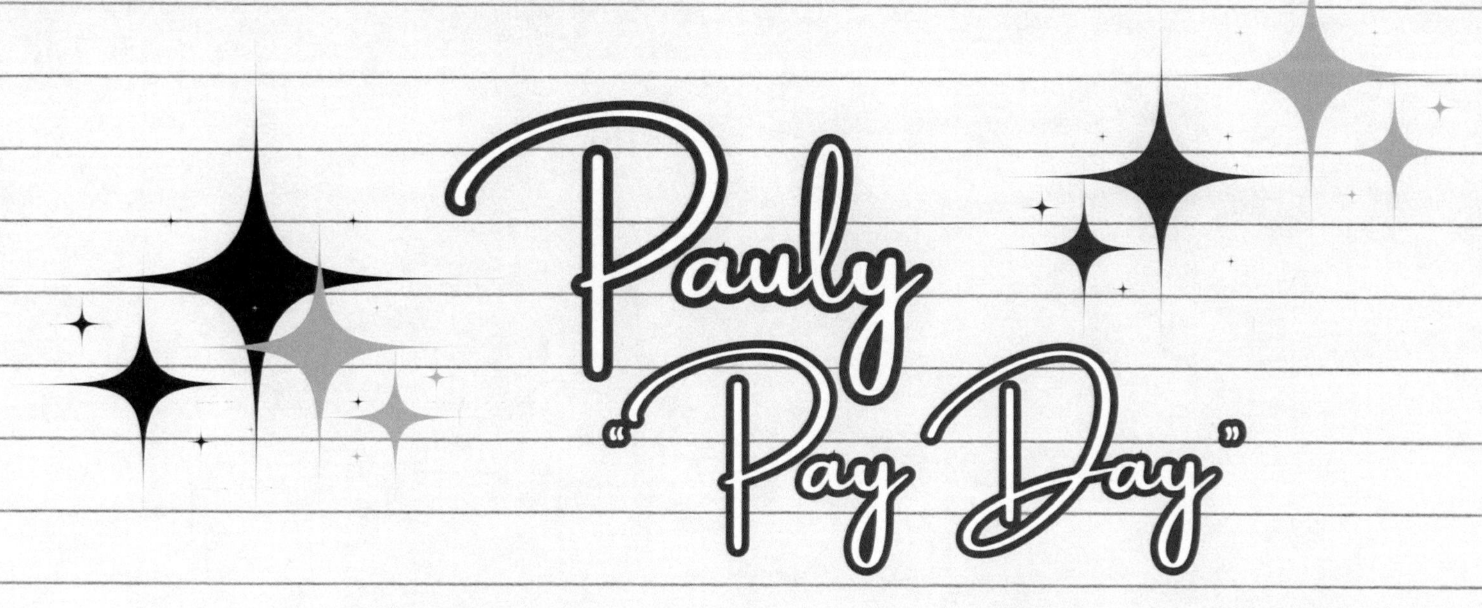

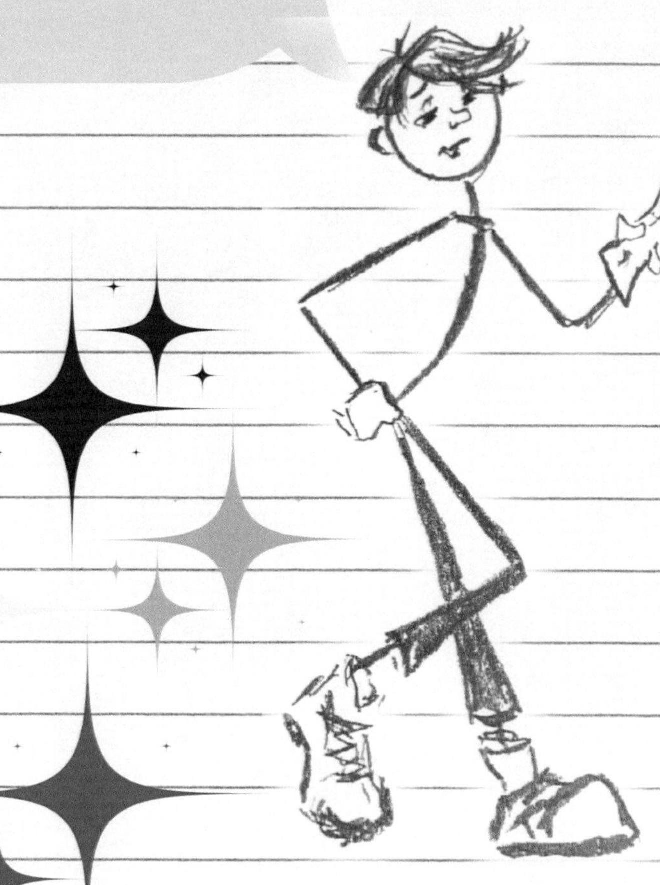

Pauly's "As long as I get paid" mindset is quite prevalent in the workplace. It's understandable that he needs to earn a living, so it's hard to fault him. After all, not everyone's job is their passion. Although this mindset may initially alleviate job related stress, it can ultimately result in lower job satisfaction and diminishing skills over time. If you're working alongside Pauly, engaging in conversations that aren't strictly work-related can sometimes boost productivity. A positive mindset fosters a productive environment.

"Don't Fire Me" Dave

In this case, Dave's lack of self-confidence has become his identity. He probably has a good reason for his fear. Perhaps, he's been bullied, humiliated, or simply struggles with fundamental skills.   Regardless of the cause, his inability to assert himself not only affects his own productivity but also burdens his teammates. A hesitant work attitude can create extra work for others, exacerbating the problem. It's crucial to recognize that there is often significant potential hidden beneath Dave's self-doubt, but he may require some encouragement and motivation. Before Dave can become effective, he must first shift his mindset to a more productive state.

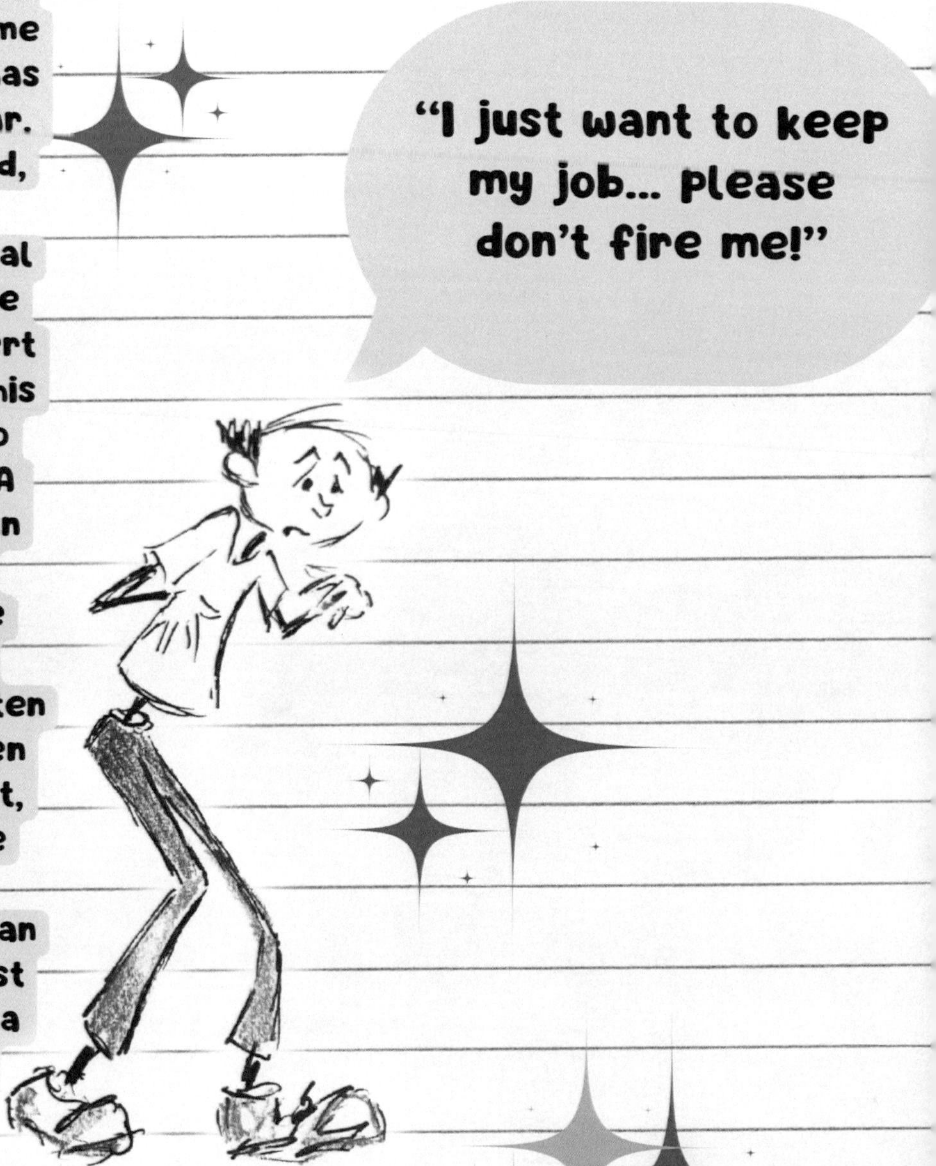

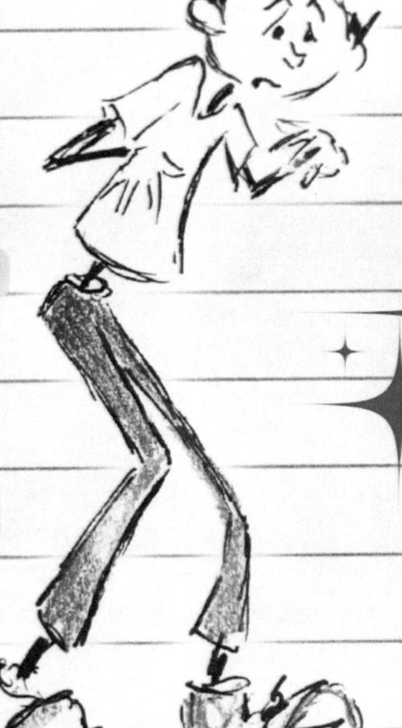

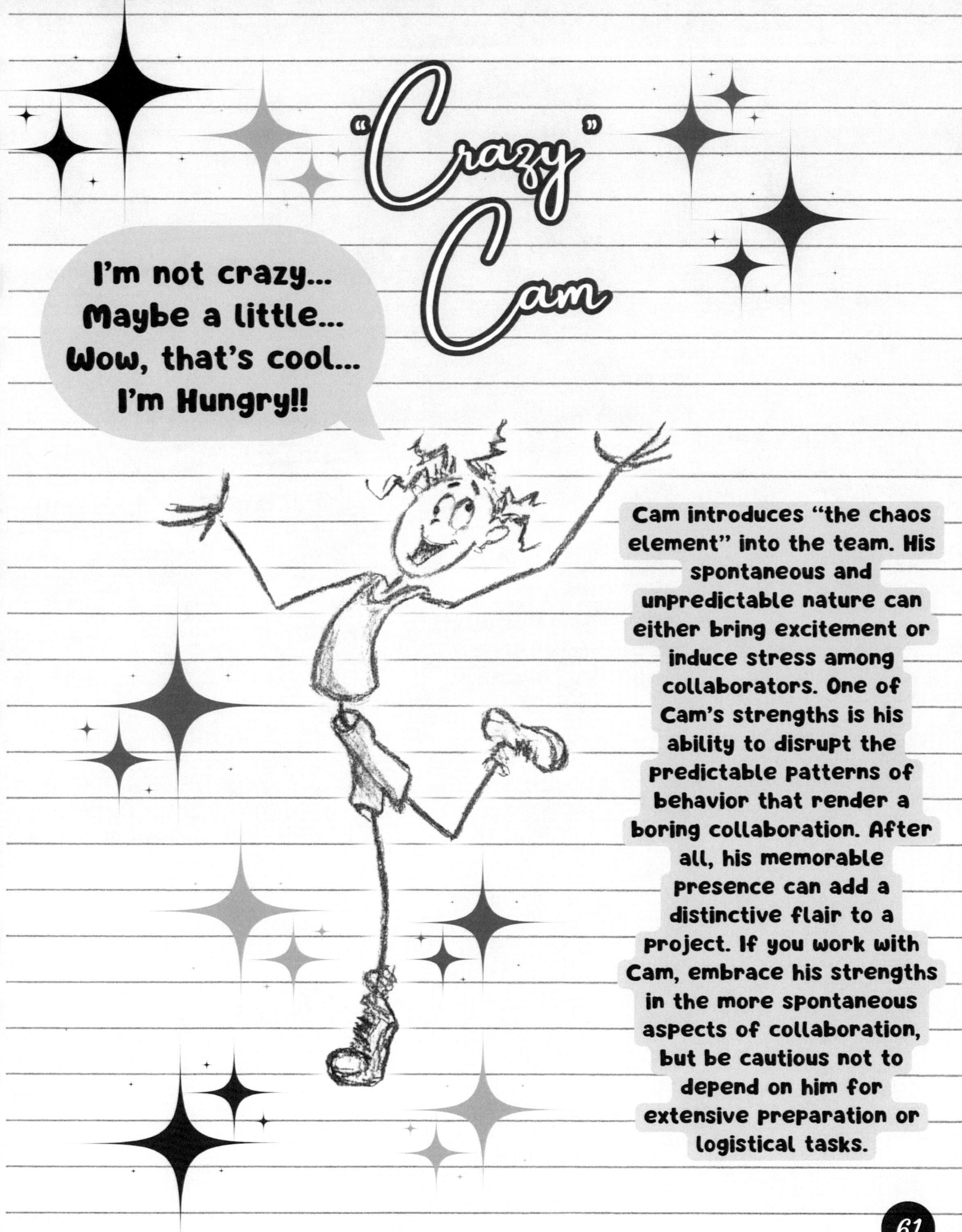

Cam introduces "the chaos element" into the team. His spontaneous and unpredictable nature can either bring excitement or induce stress among collaborators. One of Cam's strengths is his ability to disrupt the predictable patterns of behavior that render a boring collaboration. After all, his memorable presence can add a distinctive flair to a project. If you work with Cam, embrace his strengths in the more spontaneous aspects of collaboration, but be cautious not to depend on him for extensive preparation or logistical tasks.

"Lazy" Larry

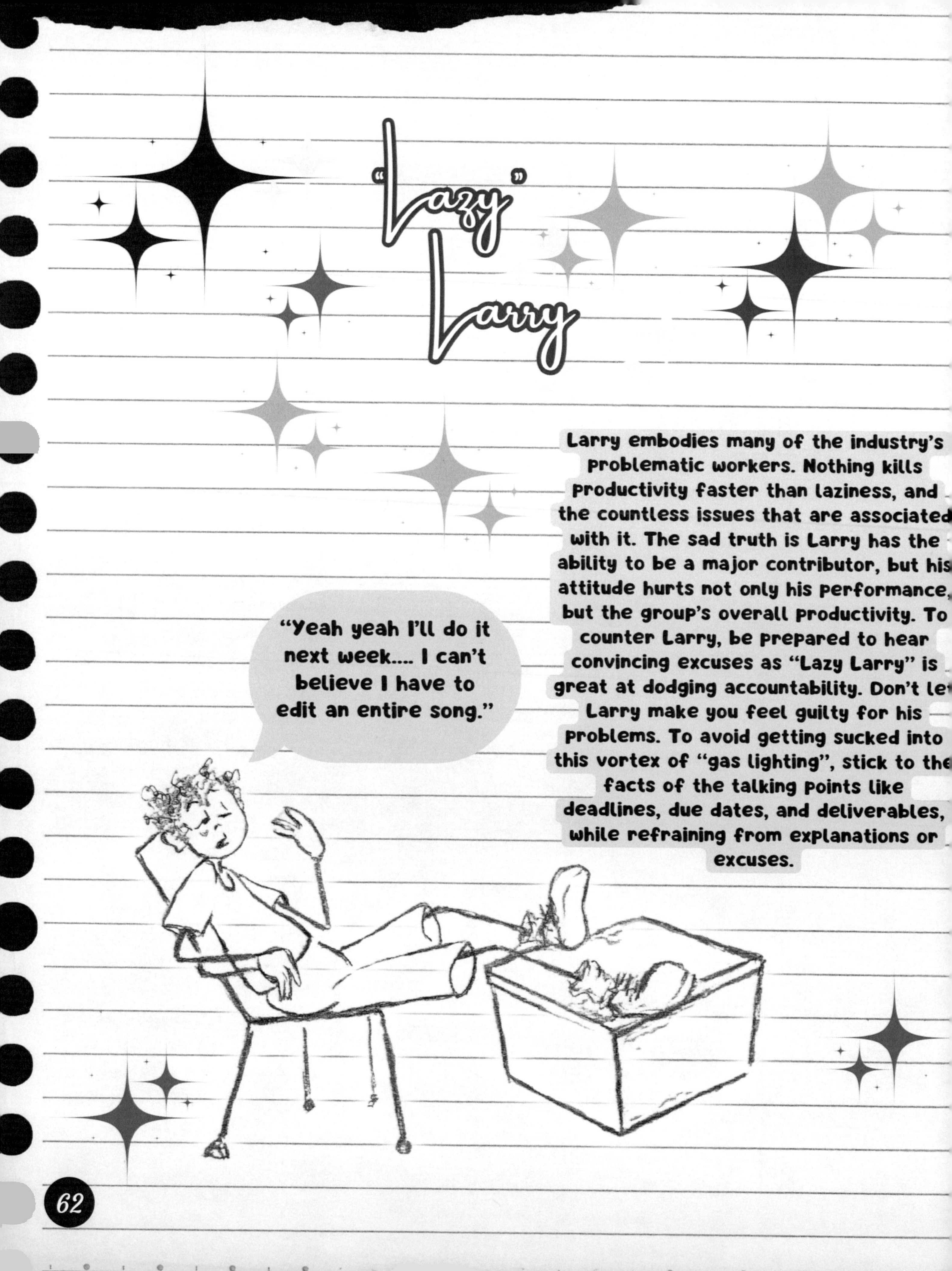

Larry embodies many of the industry's problematic workers. Nothing kills productivity faster than laziness, and the countless issues that are associated with it. The sad truth is Larry has the ability to be a major contributor, but his attitude hurts not only his performance, but the group's overall productivity. To counter Larry, be prepared to hear convincing excuses as "Lazy Larry" is great at dodging accountability. Don't let Larry make you feel guilty for his problems. To avoid getting sucked into this vortex of "gas lighting", stick to the facts of the talking points like deadlines, due dates, and deliverables, while refraining from explanations or excuses.

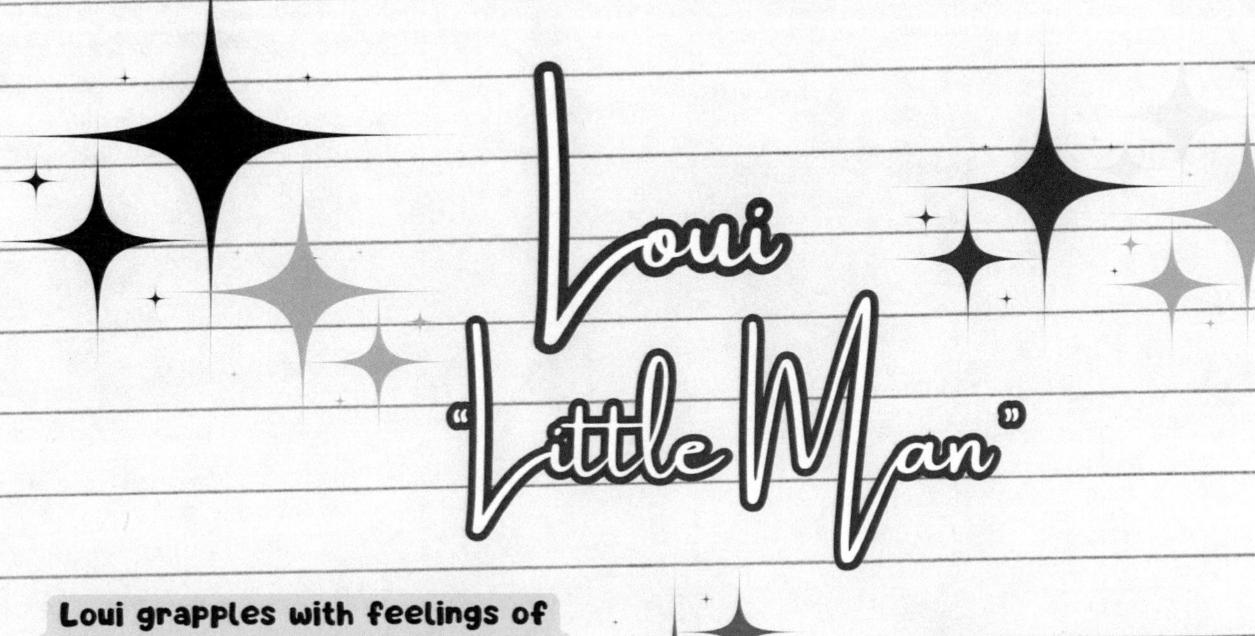

Loui grapples with feelings of inferiority. While he focuses on his height, such a complex can stem from various insecurities. Life often throws challenges our way that we cannot alter, and these burdens can weigh heavily on individuals for a lifetime. The one thing Loui can change is his mindset, though he might need support to recognize this. Like many individuals who struggle with self-confidence, affirming your respect for Loui can alleviate his feelings of inferiority. Remember, feelings of inferiority arise from a sense of being "less," so if you can help someone feel "more," it will encourage them to adopt a more constructive mindset. Occasionally, sharing some of your own insecurities can also help lessen the insecurities of others.

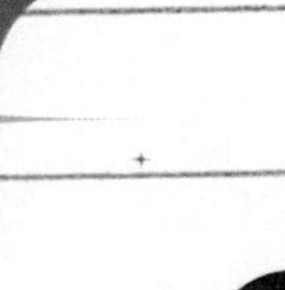

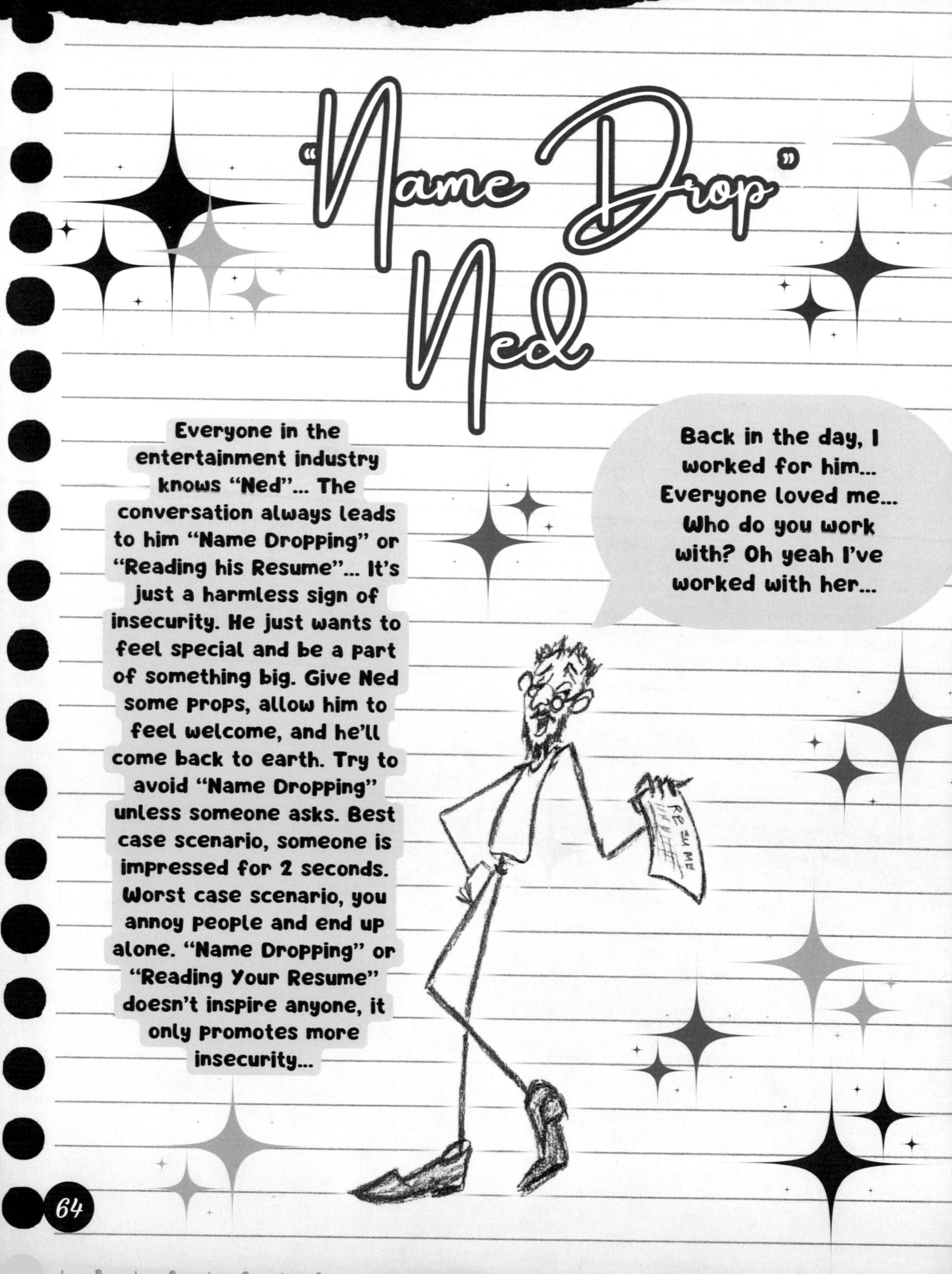

"Name Drop" Ned

Everyone in the entertainment industry knows "Ned"... The conversation always leads to him "Name Dropping" or "Reading his Resume"... It's just a harmless sign of insecurity. He just wants to feel special and be a part of something big. Give Ned some props, allow him to feel welcome, and he'll come back to earth. Try to avoid "Name Dropping" unless someone asks. Best case scenario, someone is impressed for 2 seconds. Worst case scenario, you annoy people and end up alone. "Name Dropping" or "Reading Your Resume" doesn't inspire anyone, it only promotes more insecurity...

Back in the day, I worked for him... Everyone loved me... Who do you work with? Oh yeah I've worked with her...

RESUME

Bernie "Burnout"

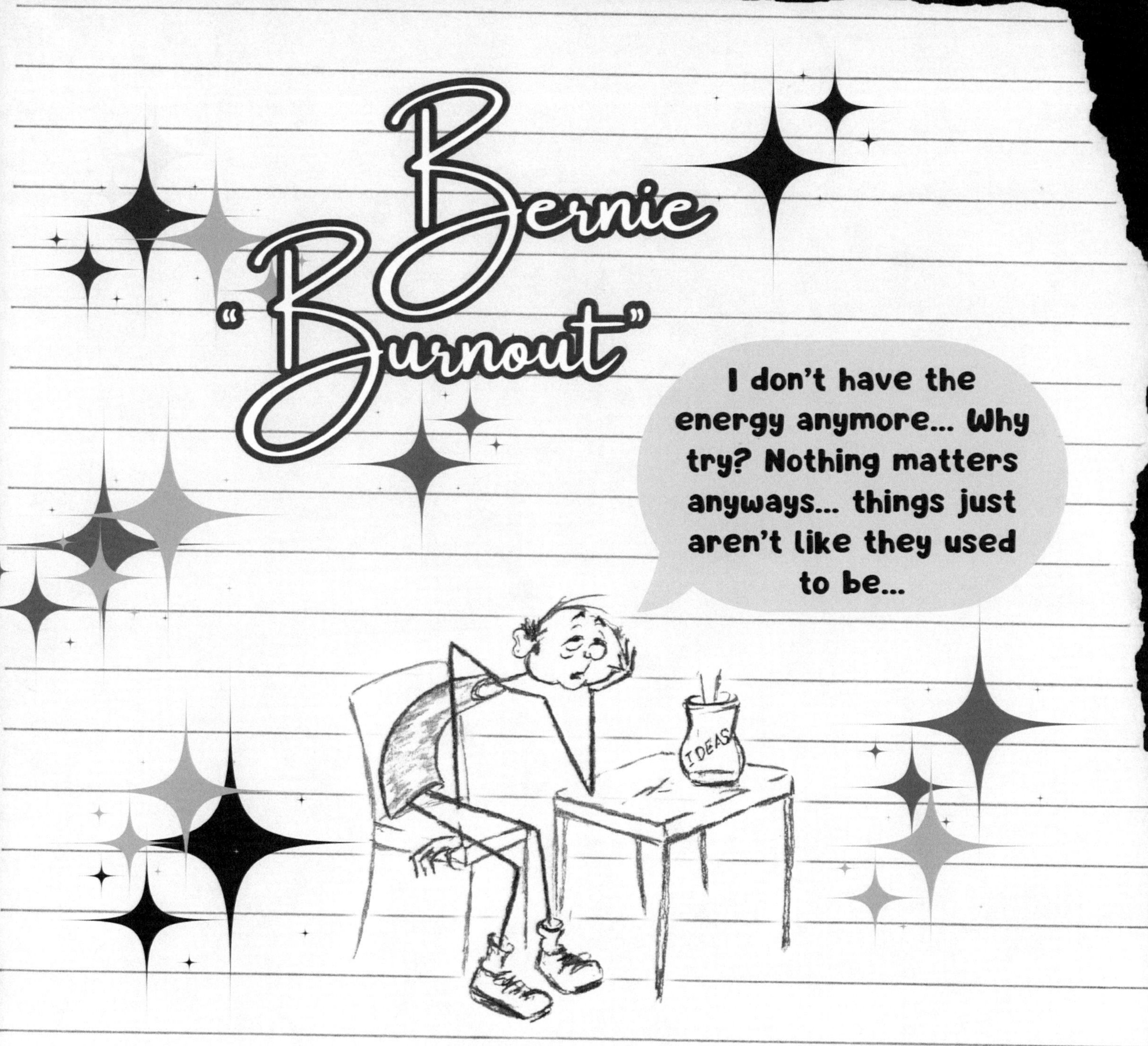

Poor Bernie... The guy has been overworked, under-appreciated, and lacking change for too many years. We all face "Burnout" at varying degrees, but Bernie's Burnout has become his identity. He wasn't always this way. He used to have a spark about him, but he doesn't quite have the energy or the sharpness to bounce back anymore. Every time he has a productive thought, it's quickly foreshadowed by self doubt or a complaint about life. There's a number of valid reason's Bernie feels this way, but ultimately he has to make a change. If you find yourself working with a "Bernie Burnout", try not to be overly energetic around them, show your appreciation for what they like, and quietly make their life easier. It might be just enough positivity for them to make a necessary change in their life.

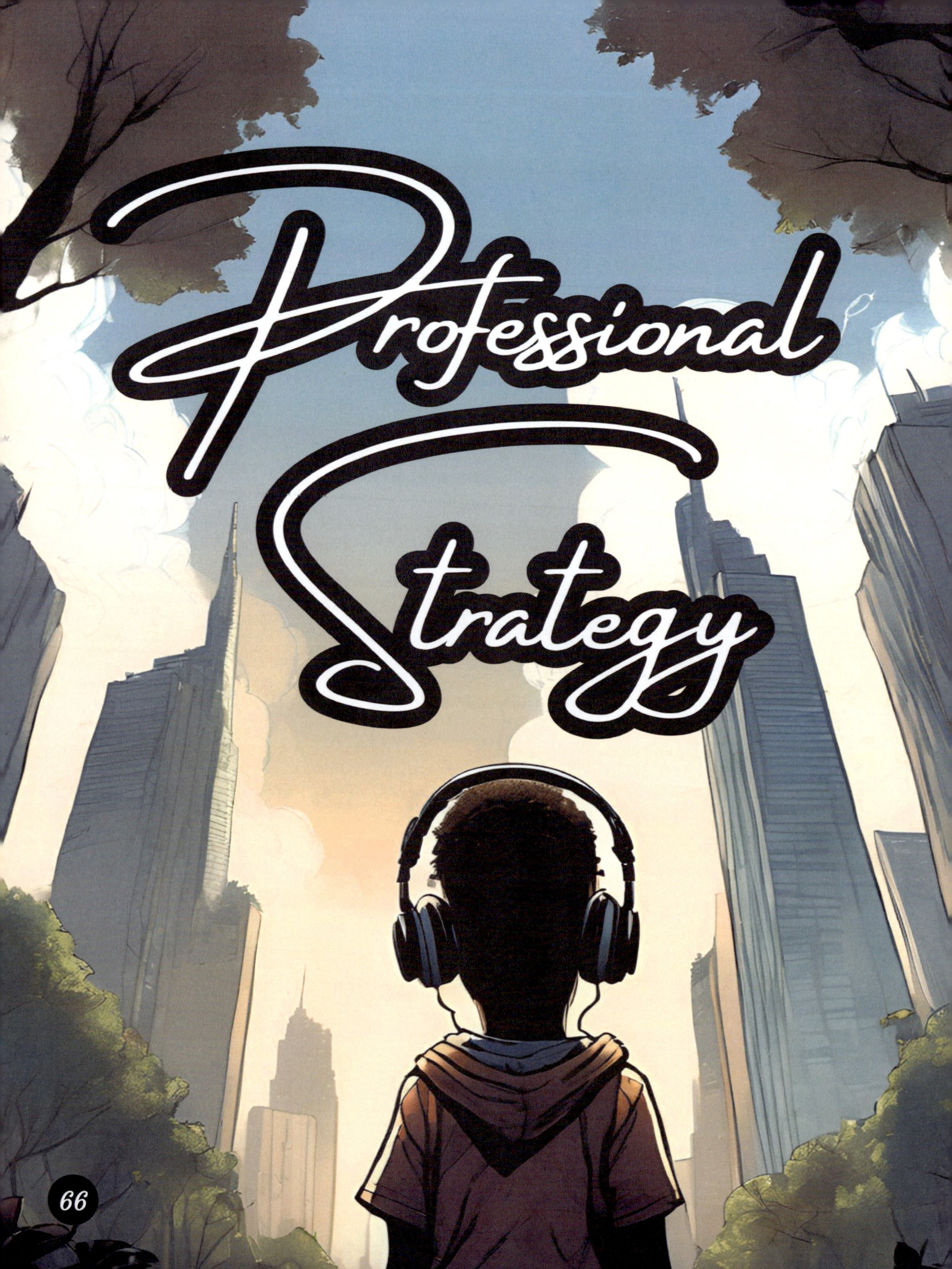
Professional
Strategy
66

Balancing the Industry

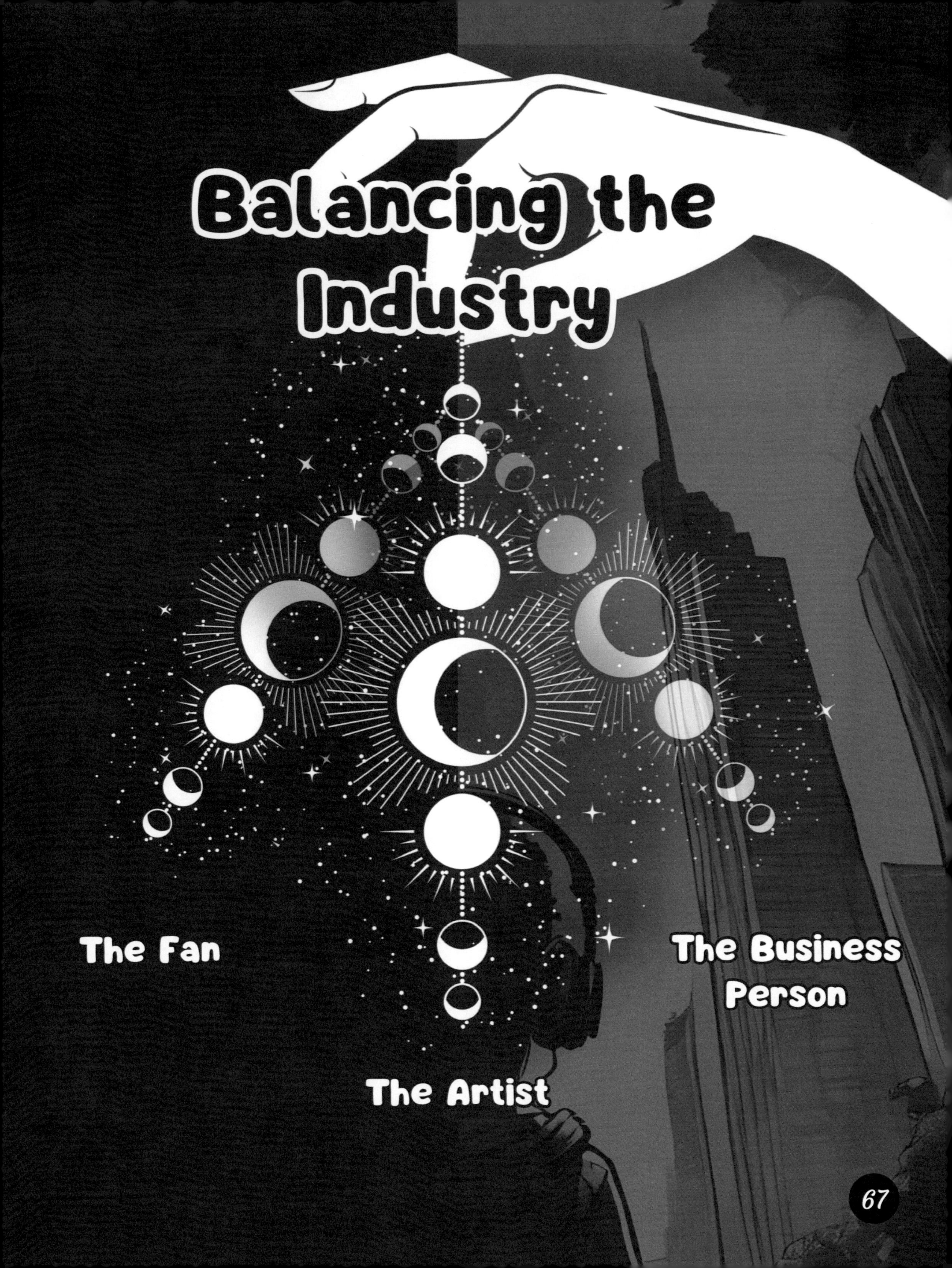

3 Fundamental Roles

Artist
(Influence / Appeal)

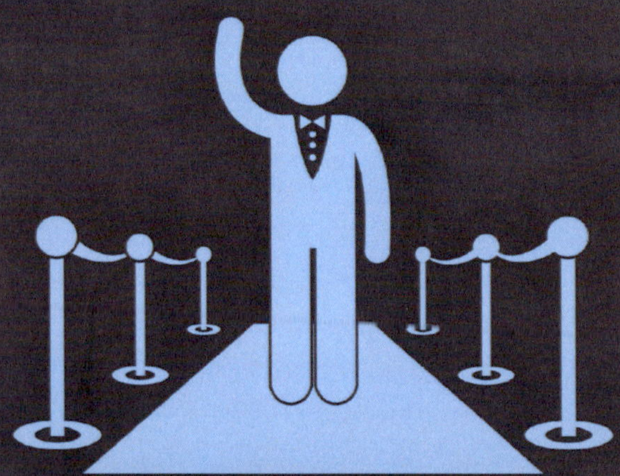

Business Person
(Structure / Resources)

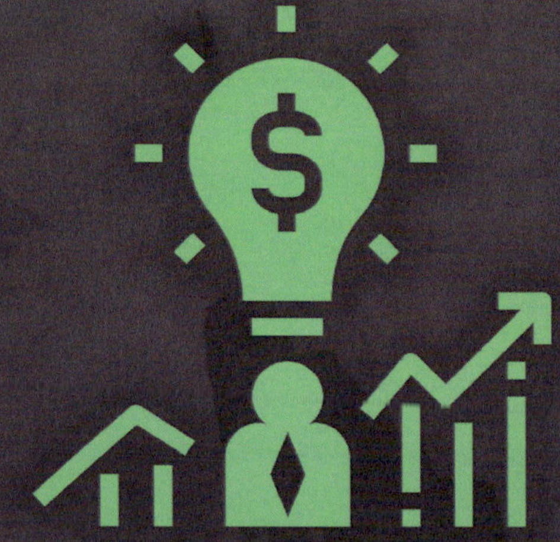

The Fan
(Consumer / Validation)

Note: The roles of both Artist and Business can be fulfilled by a sole person or delegated among a group... Both artists and business people can be fans as well.

Dependency Triangle

**Artist
(Influence / Appeal)**

**Business Person
(Structure / Resources)**

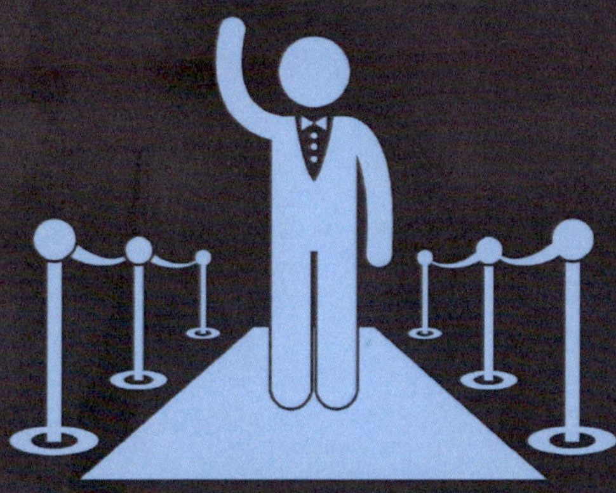

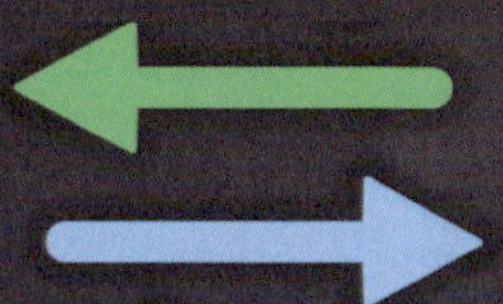

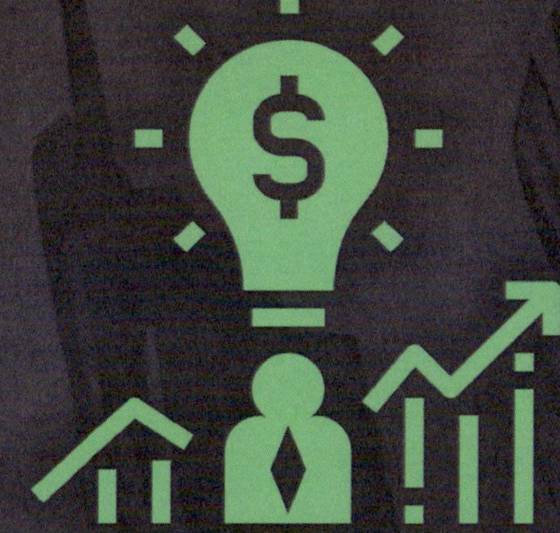

**The Fan
(Consumer / Validation)**

The Artist's Mindset

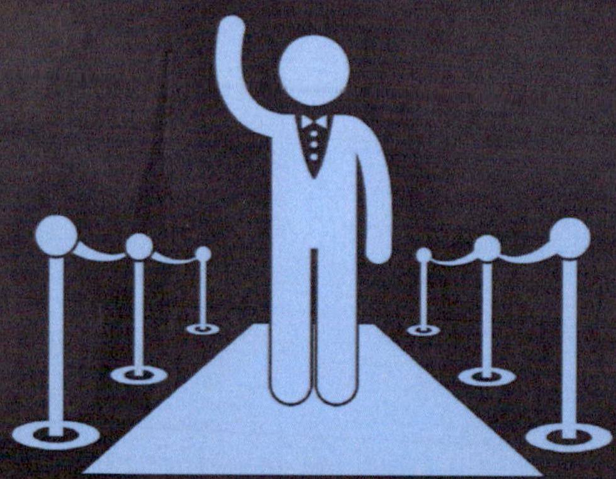

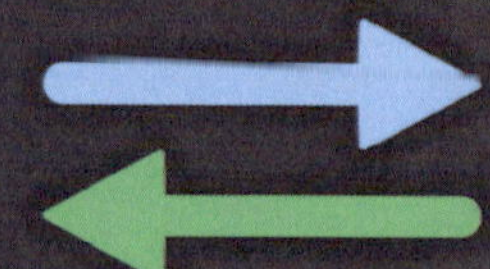

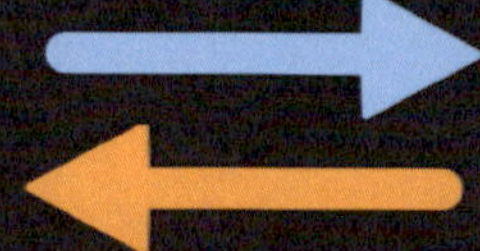

The Business Mindset

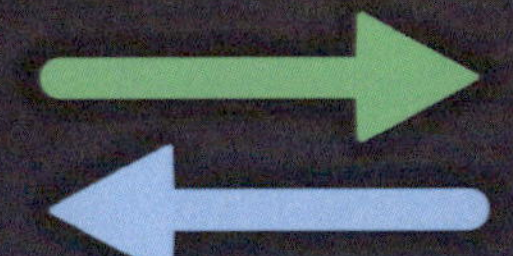

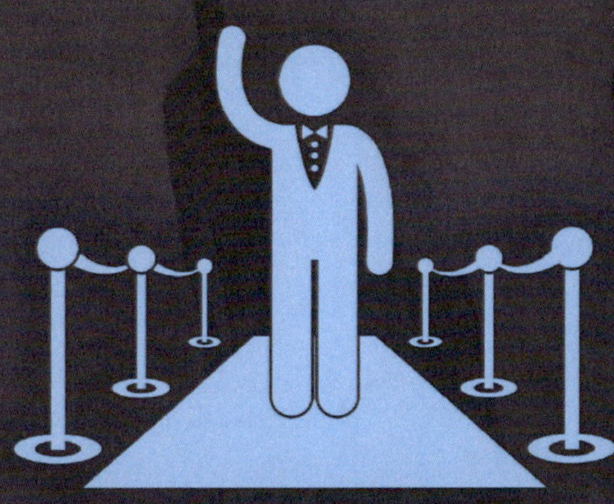

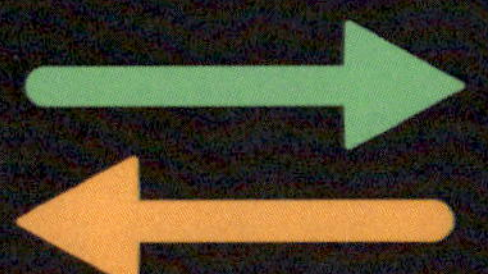

The Fan Mindset

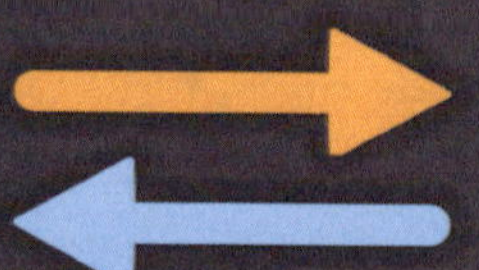

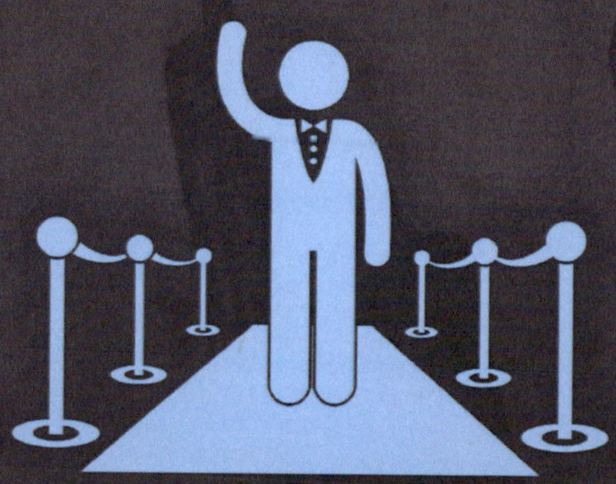

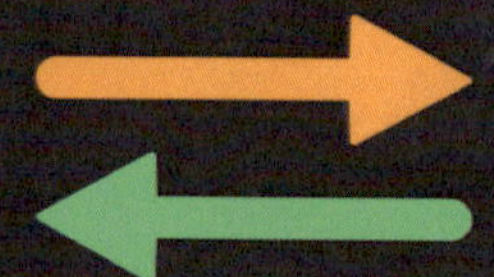

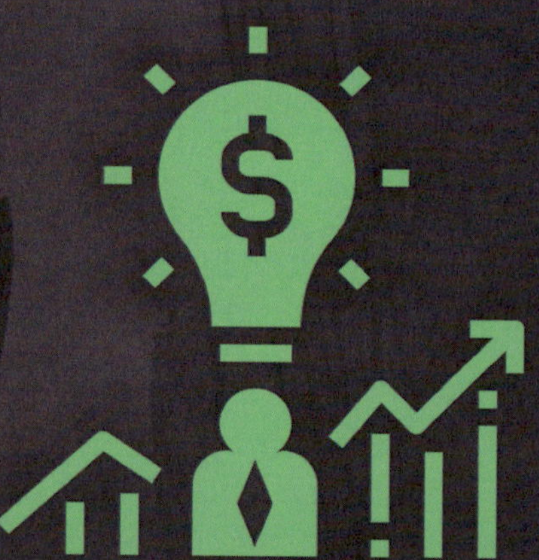

Accountability Triangle

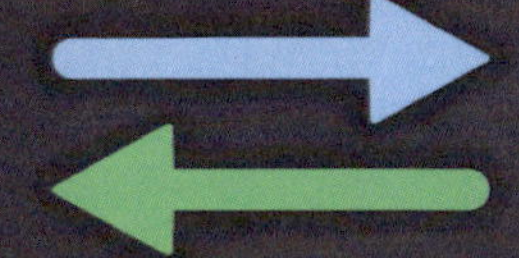

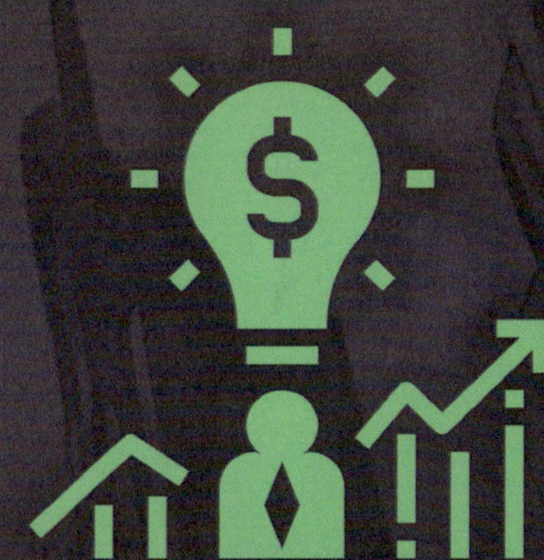

The Human Tendencies

Artists tend to lose their inspirational spark when focus shifts away from their artistry. Both the chase for fame and the pursuit of wealth can hinder an artist's growth. Ironically in this pursuit, they often make amateur business mistakes and lose popularity with their fans as the integrity of their craft diminishes.

At times business professionals can find themselves "caught up" by artistic influences, leading to unwise business decisions. In other words, a lack of discipline can lead to reckless spending and poor execution towards goals.

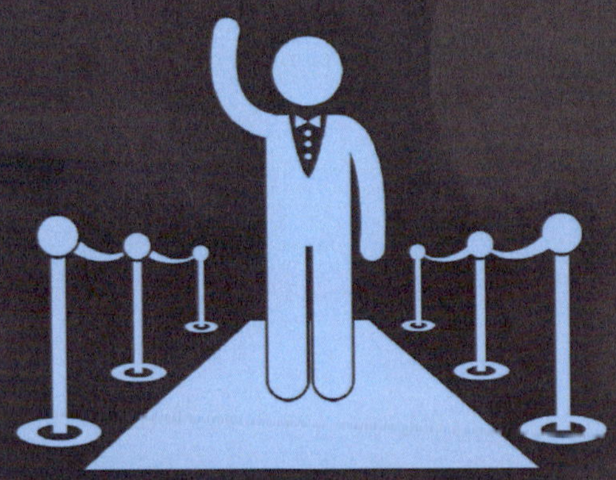

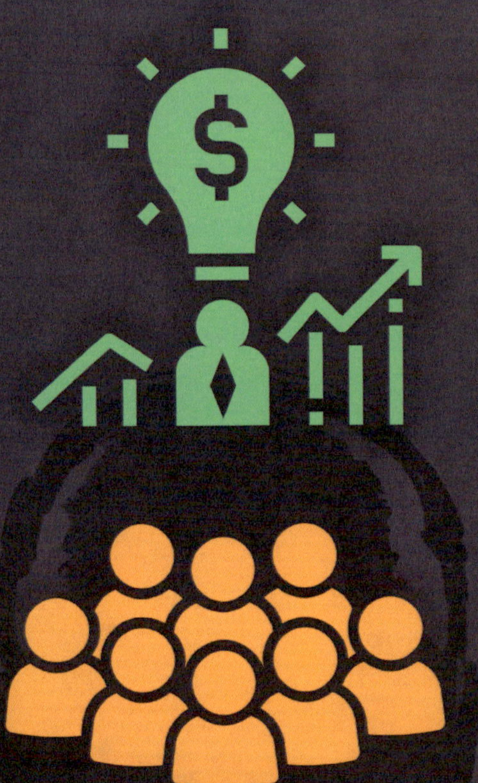

The confidence and spontaneity that is beneficial for artistic expression can sometimes conflict with structure and logical thinking. This can present challenges for productivity and organization.

When an unprofessional business encounters marginal success, members often develop a false sense of accountability in that success. In the world of entertainment it's common for these irresponsible business representatives to overstep their role within the artistic process, undermining much of the "unique" artistic elements that inspired the fans in the first place.

In today's world, where technology and social media provide endless stimulation, it's easy to adopt a passive stance regarding your entertainment choices. When a fan doesn't actively pursue inspiration, influence is decided by whomever regulates influential content released to the public. Simply put...
"IF YOU AREN'T CHOOSING WHO YOU LISTEN TO, WHO IS?"

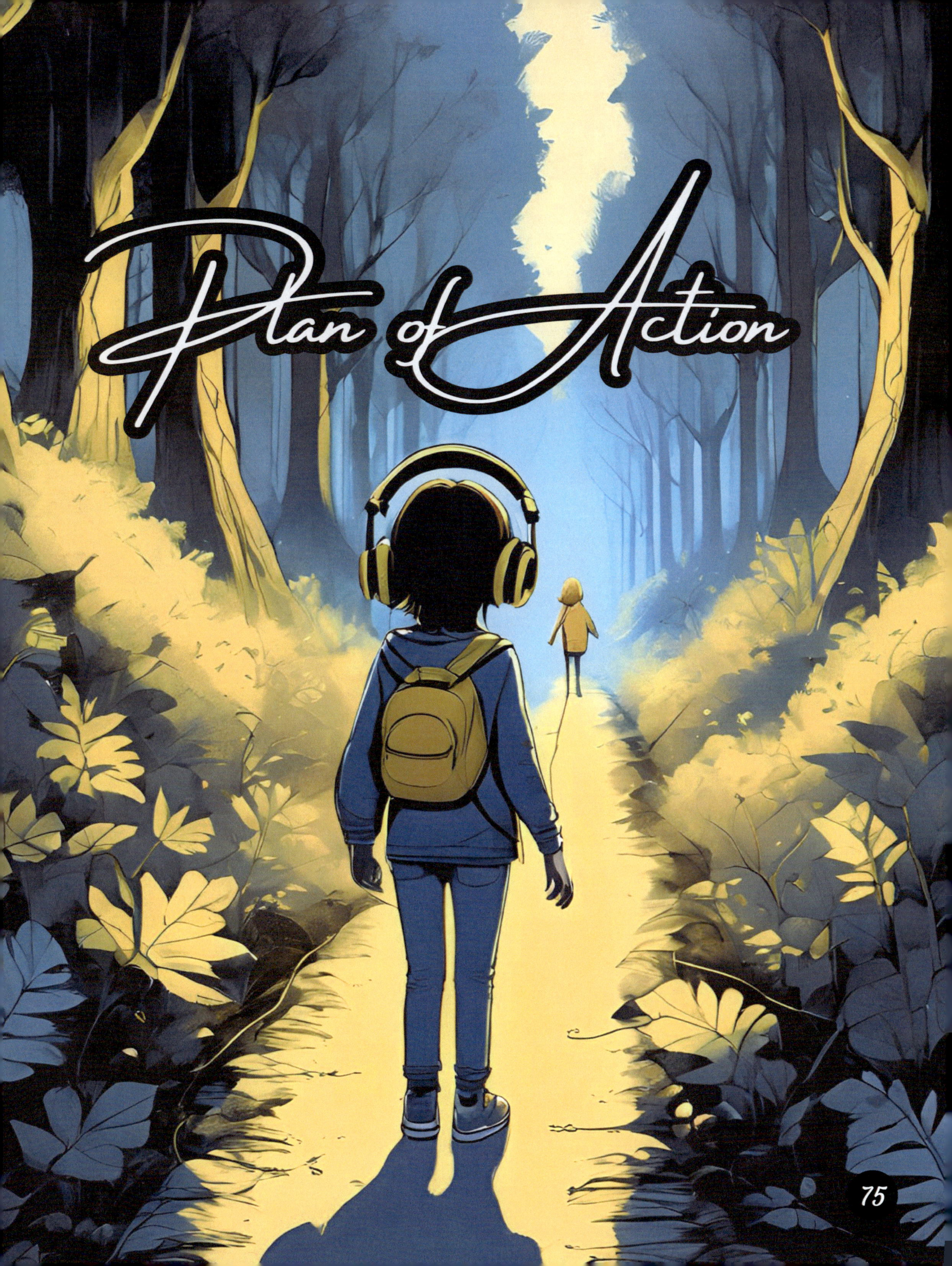
Plan of Action

"Anticipate the Project's Final Destination"

Strive to immerse yourself in the listener's context while creating. This understanding can effectively guide the creative process in a "situationally tasteful" direction. For example, if a song is going to be heard in a sports arena, imagine yourself cheering on your favorite sports team in a "loud / energetic" stadium, while creating the song. From a logistics perspective, this approach will also assist in addressing many technical and situational drawbacks beforehand. Imagine your music played in the following contexts....

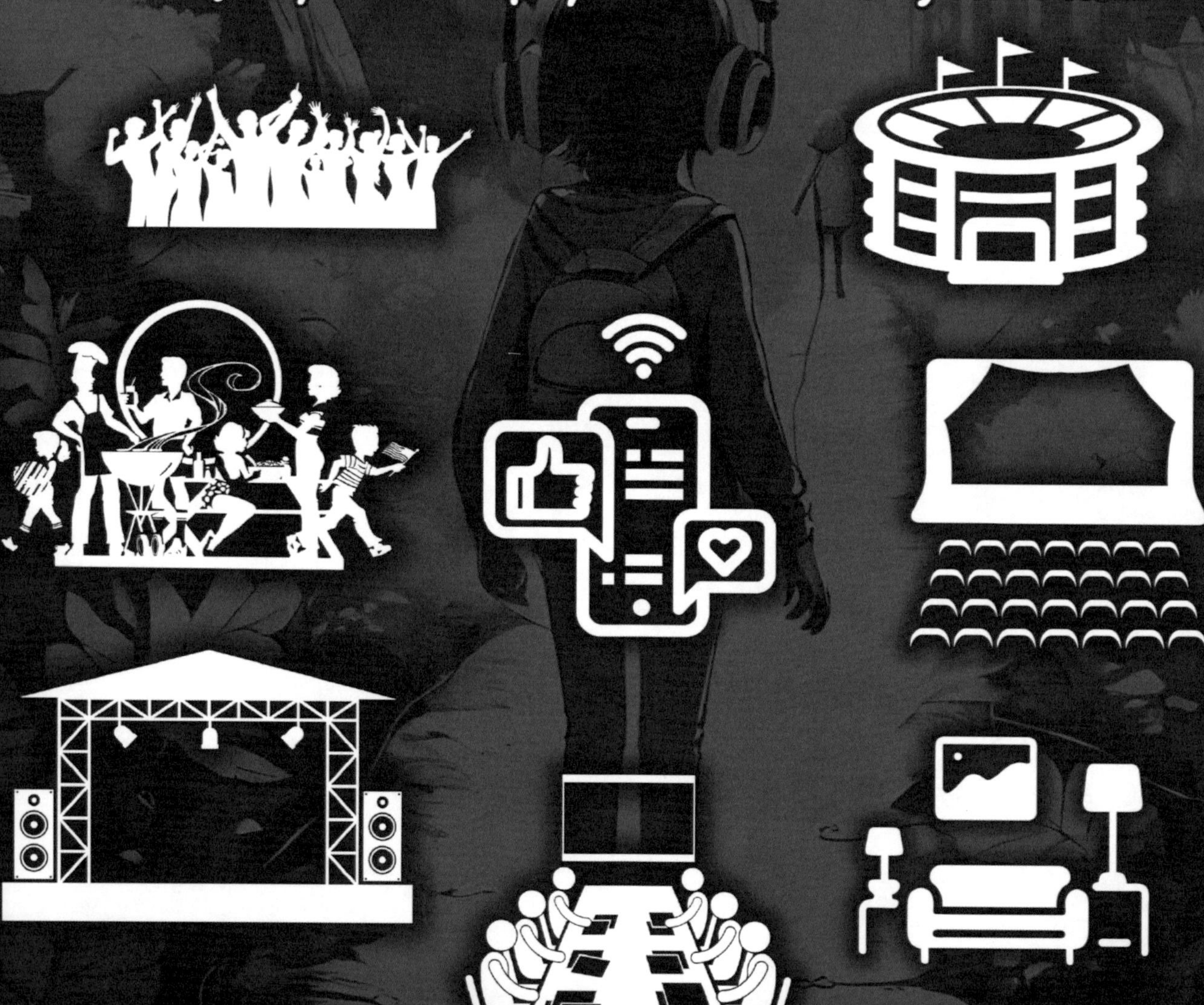

The Artist Plan of Action: Part 1
"Inspire Those You Know"

Question: How many social media friends do you have?
Answer: 100

Approach each post as if you are performing
for an audience of 100 people

Social media posts provide fans direct access
to an artist's creations

A "genuine fan base" is an artist's strongest
asset in negotiation...

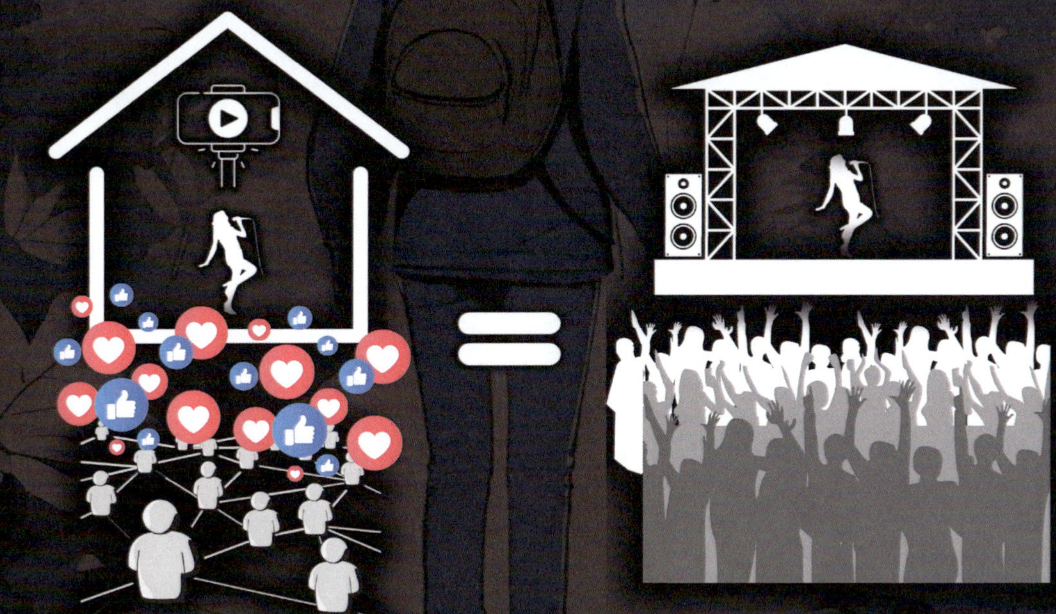

Remember! At this phase it's less about how many friends you
have, but rather how engaged are your fans with your artistry...

The Artist Plan of Action: Part 2
"Understand the Business Perspective"

As an artist it's important to understand your role in a business plan.

It can be challenging both emotionally and logistically to "objectify" artistry. However, much like a sales person, an artist has a unique ability to make a product more appealing. This is the true value that an artist brings to the business realm, and it is where much of the negotiation power lies in favor of the artist.

This is how a Purse company would see value in an artist...

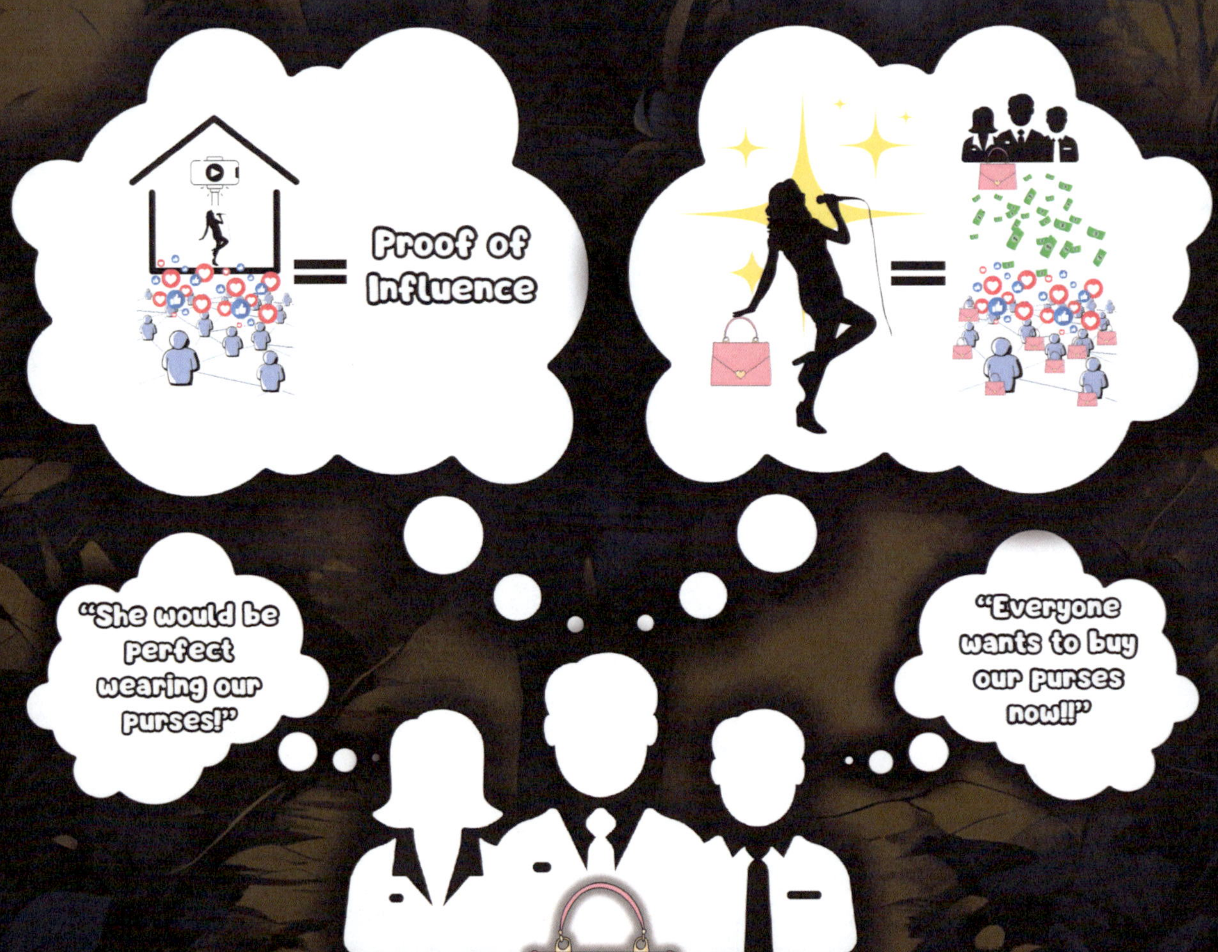

The Artist Plan of Action Part 3
"Determine Your Value"

Given the situation, use your best judgement to determine
the value of your artistic influence.

You can charge on a "per project" or "by time" basis. You can also seek residual or "back end" compensation, however in this case use your best judgment to decide if the project will profit in the long term. Be sure to seek professional legal representation regarding contracts. Also, be weary of businesses who negotiate with the talk of "big opportunities" in exchange for free services. Businesses who appreciate the value of art won't expect an artist to work for free.

Remember, it is good business to eliminate unnecessary spending, so don't take it personal that a business wants to "low ball" your artistic value. You can name your price, but be sure that you can justify your price with proof of influence.

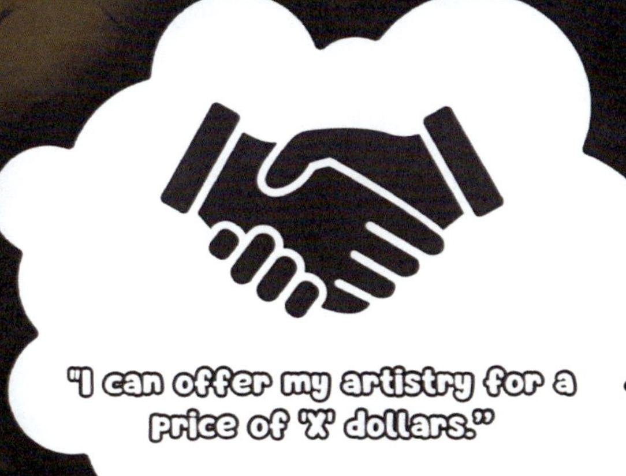

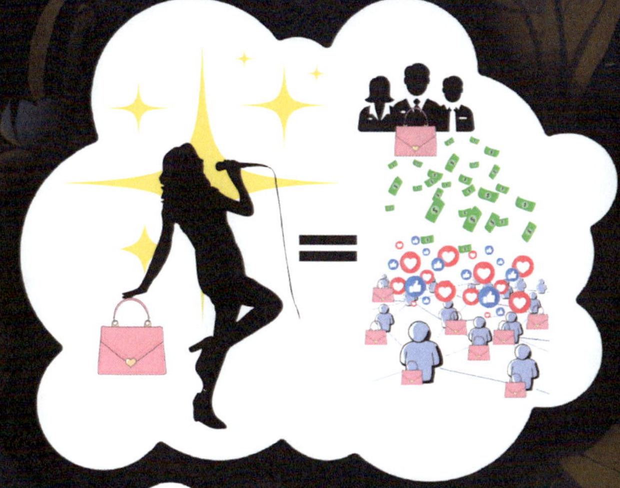

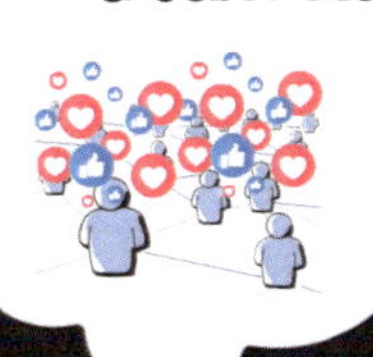

"How you value your artistry should closely resemble how others value your artistry... An imbalance will create tension in the negotiation."

The Artist Plan: Part 5
"Independent Artist"

The Independent Artist opts to operate independently, managing their own business entity without the dependence of an organization.

It's crucial to understand effective business practices and differentiate between artistic and business decisions.

This approach requires a high degree of commitment and hard work. As your business grows, think about building a team and delegating tasks. This will enable you, as the artist, to concentrate on your creative work. Keep in mind, the more successful you are as an artist, the more dependent you will become on others to manage your business.

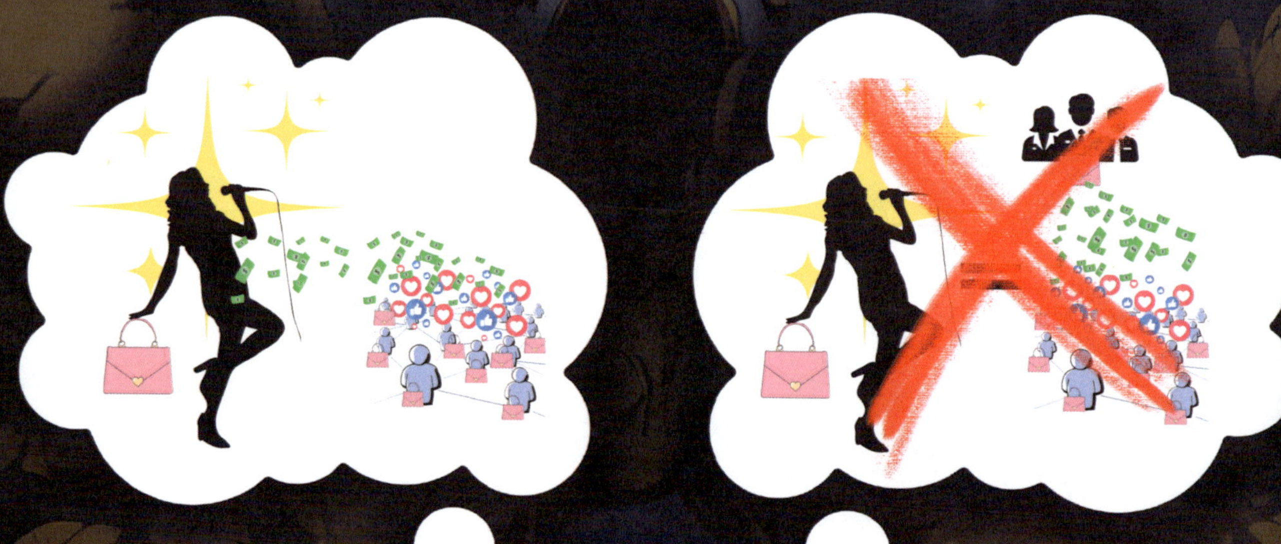

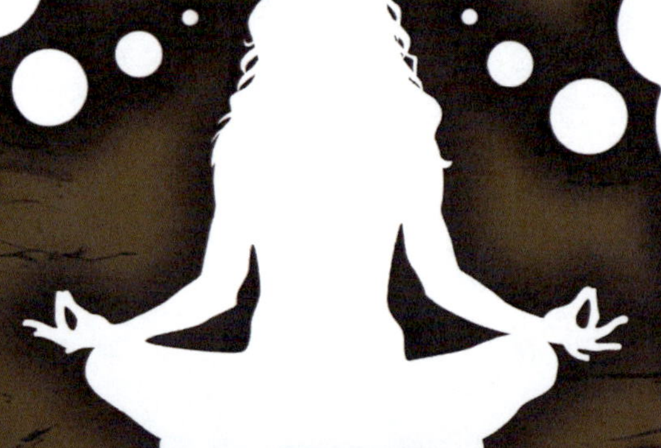

The Artist Plan: Part 4
"Record Label or Production Company"

When collaborating with a record label, negotiation is essential, just as it is in any other industry. However, the key advantages lie in the access to artistic resources that far exceed what traditional companies can provide.

Major record labels have established enduring relationships with experienced promoters, marketers, and distributors, which are essential for reaching a broader audience. Cultivating these connections can simplify the path to achieving substantial visibility through a record deal, although this increased exposure often comes with compromises, such as ownership stakes and royalty agreements.

Beyond securing a record deal, having distinctive skills and creativity is crucial for various roles within a production company or record label. Keep in mind that labels are always on the lookout for the next "big thing," so be ready to impress them with your authentic talent and influence.

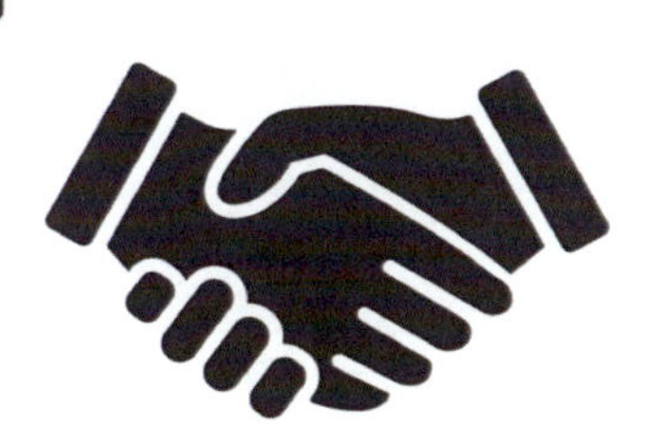

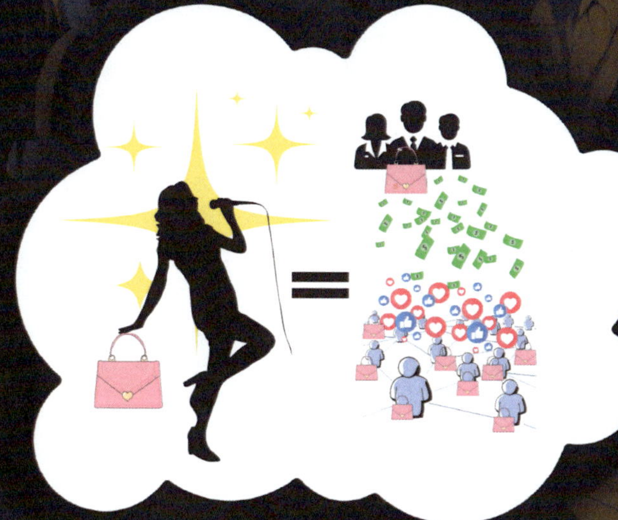

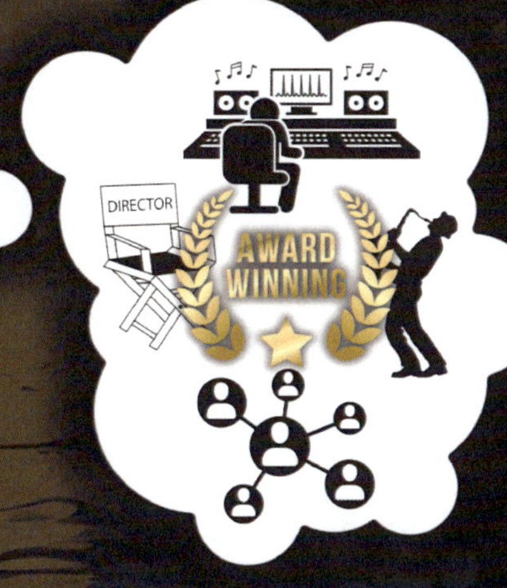

Living in The Pendulum Process

As we wrap up our journey here in "The Pendulum Process," keep in mind the importance of "balancing your life." These three values complement each other, yet often appear to conflict in everyday scenarios. It won't be simple, but aim to find harmony between your personal and professional life, as overlooking any of these values can impede your sense of fulfillment throughout life's journey.

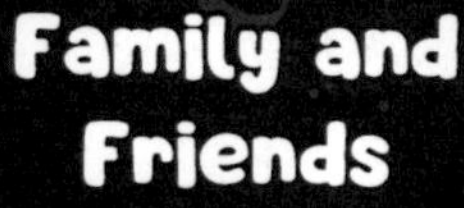

Family and Friends

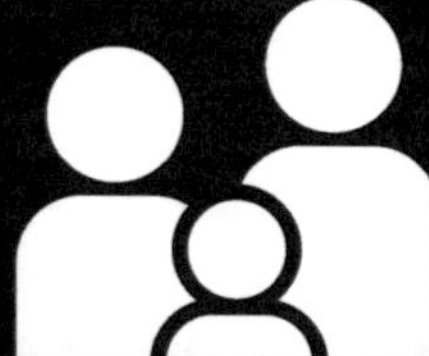

Health and Wellbeing

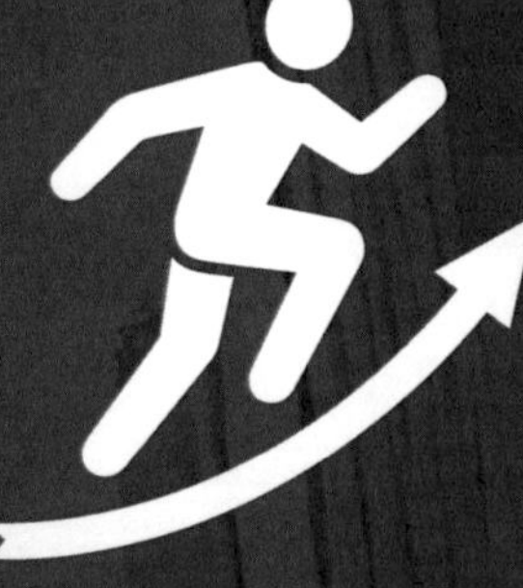

Career and Ambition